WATERCOLOUR
TIPS & TRICKS

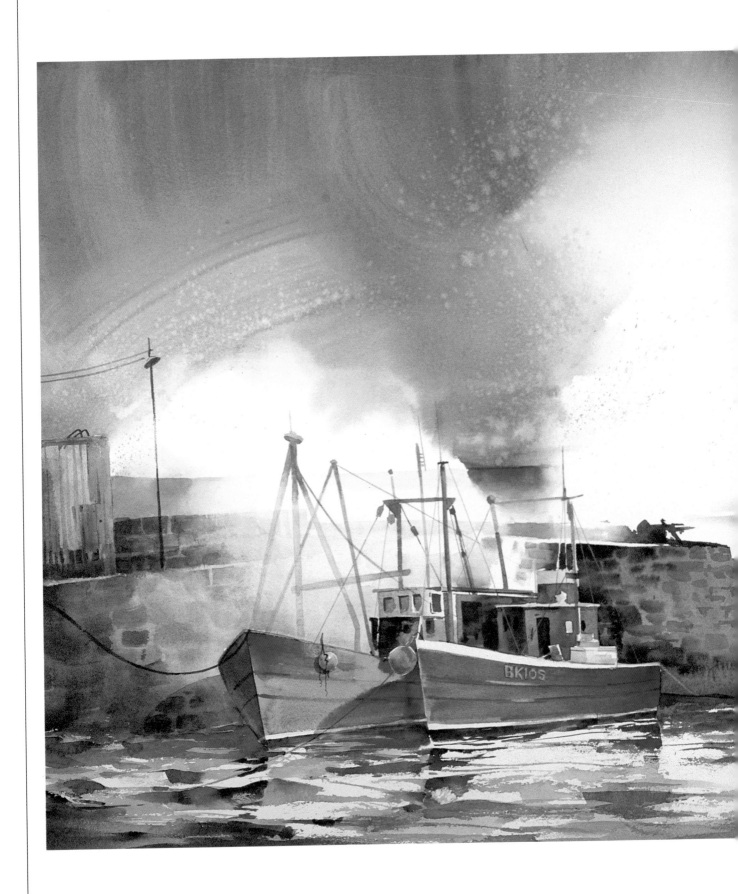

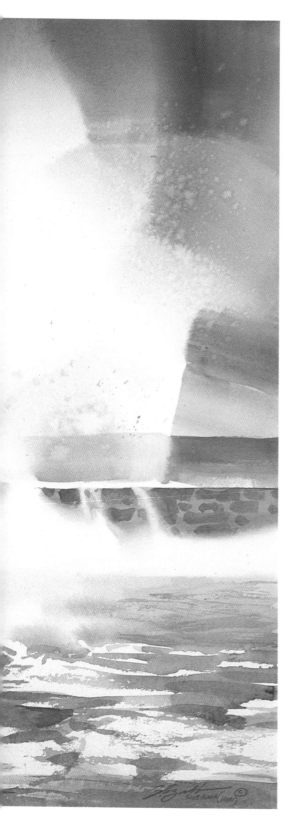

WATERCOLOUR
TIPS & TRICKS

OVER **70** ESSENTIAL
TECHNIQUES FOR PAINTING
LANDSCAPE SUBJECTS

Zoltan Szabo

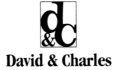

David & Charles

A DAVID & CHARLES BOOK

First published in the UK in 1997
First published in the USA in 1995 by North Light Books, Cincinnati, Ohio

A catalogue record for this book is available from the British Library.

ISBN 0 7153 0547 6

Printed in Hong Kong by Midas Printing Ltd
for David & Charles
Brunel House   Newton Abbot   Devon

For information on ordering the art supplies mentioned in this book
please write to:
      Zoltan Szabo
      Watercolor Workshops
      1220 Glenn Valley Drive
      Matthews, NC 28105
For information on art instruction videos by Zoltan Szabo
please write to the same address.

Dedication

This book represents my sincere desire to transfer some of the knowledge that I have accumulated through forty-five years of painting and teaching to those who wish to benefit from it. During this period there were rough times when, just like many of you, I felt lost and the value of my efforts seemed at least questionable. I am proud to claim six wonderful Canadian friends who helped me through the roughest time early in my career. They are Keith R. Shadlock, Frank J. Robinson, Lawrie R. Kingsland and their wonderful wives, Eleanor, Joan and Anne. Because of their efforts my future as an artist obtained a second chance. For their faith in my work and for their unselfish help when I needed it most, I gratefully dedicate this book to them.

Acknowledgments

A volume of this complexity would not be possible to produce without the help of many dedicated and skilled companions. Willa McNeill and Jack Richeson are two of these dear friends whose steadfast encouragement, advice, support and unconditional help greatly contributed to the completion of this book.

Rachel Wolf, acquisition editor, in particular, Kathy Kipp, my editor, and Angela Lennert, the designer, with their professional skill, devotion and cheerful cooperation made my job not only easier but truly a pleasure. To them and to all who helped I offer my humble gratitude.

Contents

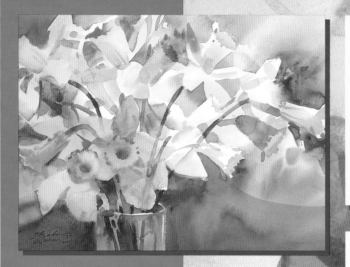

Introduction

It is my hope and desire that this book will help to further the technical advancement of young watercolour artists. I use the term 'young' intentionally because age has nothing to do with experience or attitude. If you are a novice watercolourist you are young even if you happen to be a senior citizen.

In any endeavour, knowledge combined with experience and tenacity is the key to success. Knowledge about watercolour is readily attainable through study. Throughout the following pages I will show you how easy it is to paint with watercolours after you have familiarized yourself with just a few techniques. This collection of techniques is based on solutions to problems that have confronted most of my students during my thirty years of teaching watercolour workshops.

Watercolour Pigments

A common mystery to the vast majority of students is the nature of transparent watercolour pigments. In this book I include a chapter designed to shed clear light on the subject and dispel most of the confusion.

Design

Another area in which students are often lacking is a simple and basic knowledge of design. Unfortunately, this subject sounds very scientific, which translates into 'no fun'. This does not have to be true. In the chapter on composition and design I explain some simple and easy-to-use principles that will creatively spark your design awareness.

Reflections

I find that many watercolourists paint water because they love this beautiful and intriguing subject. However, when it comes to painting reflections on the water, they get flustered and sometimes discouraged because they are not

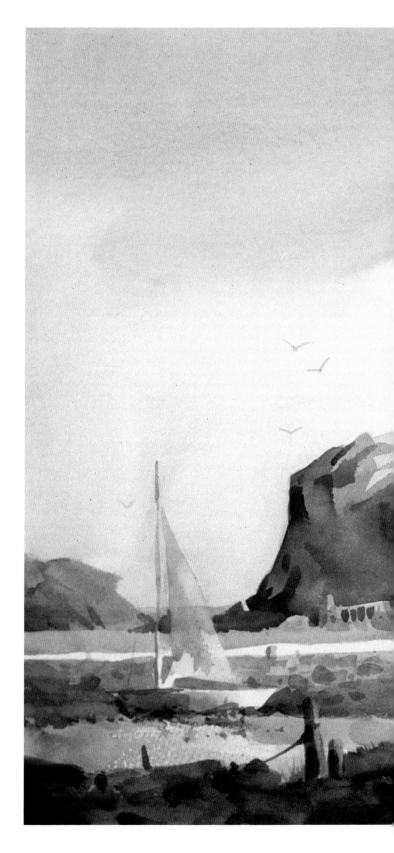

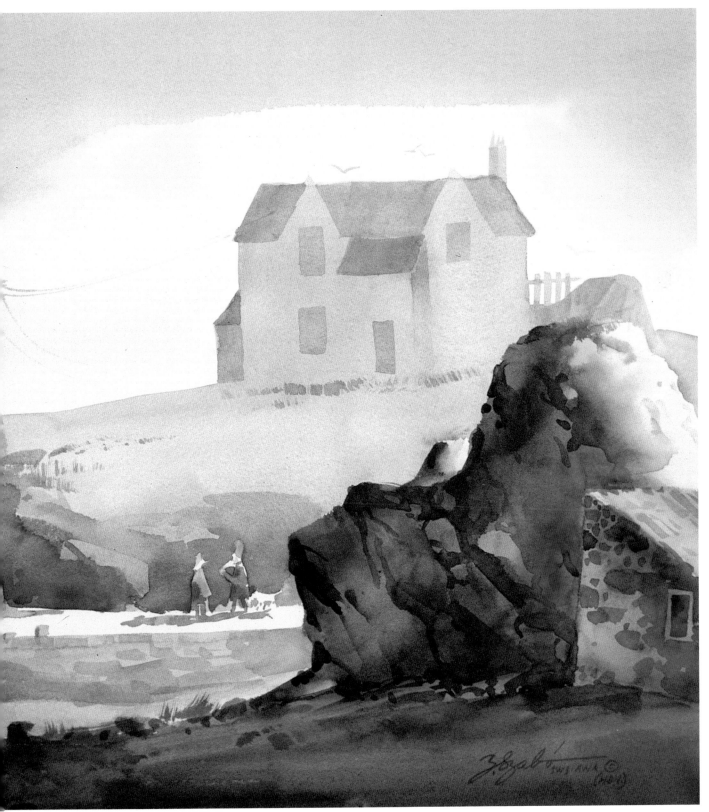

Low Tide
34.25x44.5cm (13½x17½in)

familiar with the physical laws of reflection. Even those artists who take licence and paint a strongly abstracted design will paint a more convincing painting if the reflections feel right. To a representational artist, this knowledge is essential. My chapter on reflections comes to the rescue, should you need any help with this subject.

Popular Techniques

Because the technical behaviour of water-colour is so varied, I have included many quick watercolour sketches to show you some of the most exciting and popular techniques that I use in my paintings. These examples, on pages 54 to 109, are not finished paintings but small informative sketches to explain particular technical points. You are free to copy them. They will also help you make sure that the tools you choose will behave well in your hands. In other words, I want you to master these techniques in the shortest possible time and enjoy the experience while you are learning.

Demonstrations

The last section in this book shows you many of the above principles and pointers applied in actual demonstration paintings. These paintings are shown in progress with step-by-step photographs of the works as they evolve.

I don't claim that everything you need to know about watercolour is in this or any other book. Watercolour is too fickle a medium to be explained so easily. However, I believe that, based on the material in this book, you can quickly reach a high level of technical efficiency. How far you will go with it will depend on your perseverance. Franz Liszt, the great composer and piano virtuoso, said 'If I don't practise for one day I can tell the difference the next day. If I don't practise for two days my audience can also tell the difference.' You don't

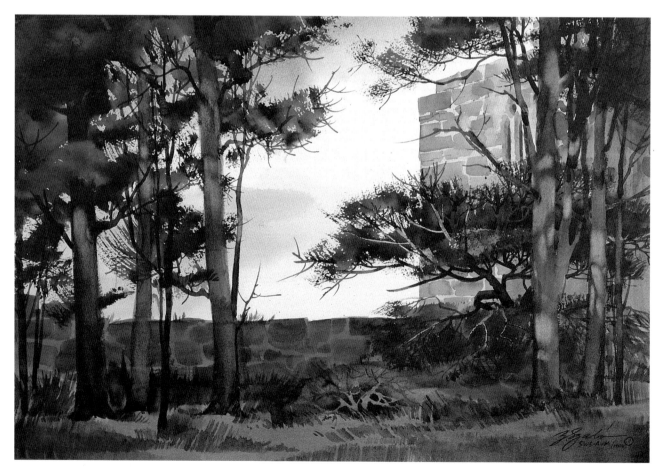

Light on History
34.25x44.5cm (13½'x17½in)

have to take this hint literally to be a good watercolourist (unless you want to paint as well as Liszt played the piano). Few people paint every single day. Nevertheless, the more often you paint the easier it gets.

To make this book fun and easy to use, I am presenting the techniques in many short, illustrated sections to allow you to *see* what I'm talking about and to enable you to use this book either as a reference volume or as a complete study guide.

Once you've gained the necessary skill, you'll be able to express your ideas and visions well enough to share them with the rest of humanity. Then you will invent your own new approaches to watercolour, and will virtually eliminate problems because you will be able to adjust and correct as you paint.

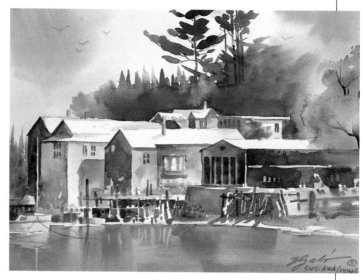

Oregon Harbor
27.5x37cm (11x14½in)

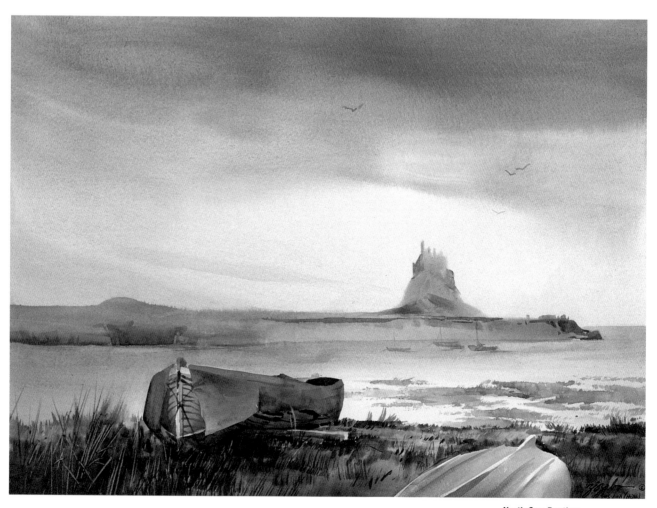

North Sea Bastion
34.25x44.5cm (13½'x17½in)

My Favourite Tools

Brushes

I have designed my own slant bristle brushes made from natural firm bristles in a variety of sizes ranging from 2.5cm (1in) to 10cm (4in), and enjoy using them for rich dark colours. The soft slant brushes 3.75cm (1½in) and 6.25cm (2½in) are also my own design and are most useful for delicate, light and wet washes. I also use a No. 5 rigger brush, a 2cm (¾in) flat, soft-hair brush, and a palette knife. As an alternative to slant brushes, broad, flat, square-cut brushes with short bristles, or hake brushes in the same sizes can be used.

Papers

My favourite papers are 640gsm (300lb). cold-pressed Lana Aquarelle (French), 640gsm (300lb) cold-pressed Arches (French), and my newest treasured discovery is Noblesse (from Holland) made by Papierfabriek Shut Bv.

I use the 640gsm (300lb) weights strictly for convenience because heavy papers don't buckle like the thinner ones when they are wet. But heavy papers soak up more paint than the thin ones, so you have to compensate for the loss of colour by painting a little richer.

Watercolour boards are also available in a range of sizes. The paper is mounted on a heavy rag board so that it doesn't buckle. The mounting material between the paper and the board keeps the water from penetrating too deep into the board, so the colours stay very intense. The result is a flat, workable surface and a high degree of colour survival.

Slant Bristle Brushes
A 7.5cm (3in)
B 5cm (2in)
C 2.5cm (1in)

Soft Slant Brushes
D 6.25cm (2½in)
E 3.75cm (1½in)

Broad Flat Brush
F 3.75cm (1½in)

Soft Flat Brush
G 2cm (¾in)

Other Brushes
H No. 2 bright oil brush
I No. 5 rigger

Palette Knife
J No. 814 Richeson

Watercolour Paints
K Winsor & Newton
L Maimeri
M Blockx

Palette with Lid
N Zoltan Szabo

Brush Blotter
O Made from toilet paper wrapped in paper towel

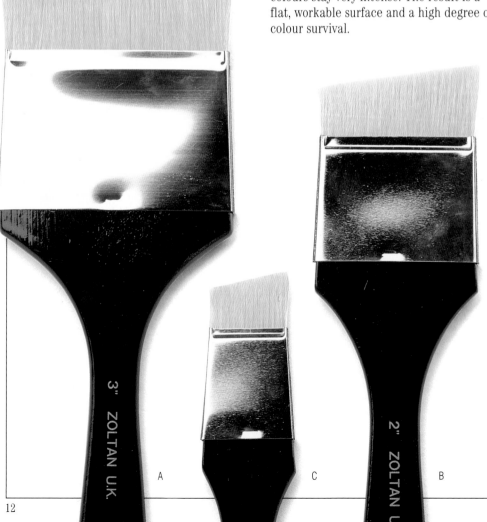

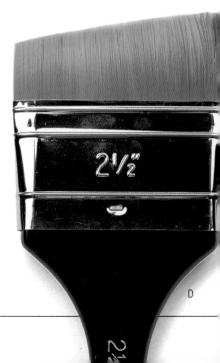

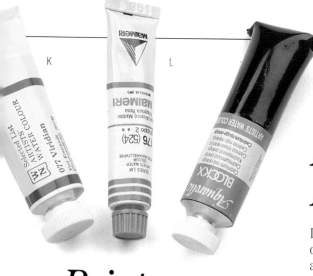

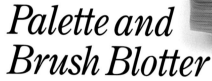

Paints

Most of the time I use three brands of top-quality transparent watercolours, though I've enjoyed painting with a few others as well—Lukas, Da Vinci, Rowney, Holbein, just to name a few. My first choice is Maimeri, then Blockx, and of course, Winsor & Newton. All three are old, proven and reliable companies and their products are consistently of the highest quality. They honestly declare the permanency level of all colours in their literature. In the case of Maimeri and Blockx, all their colours are declared permanent. Winsor & Newton also call most of their colours very permanent. However, because Winsor & Newton also serves the commercial art field (where permanency is not essential), they make some semi-permanent colours as well as a few outright fugitive pigments. It's good practice to check the declared permanency level of any colour of any brand before you fall in love with it. I will elaborate further on some of the idiosyncrasies of my favourite group of colours later, on pages 24–25.

Palette and Brush Blotter

I use a plastic palette with a lid of my own design. I squeeze out my colours in advance and let them dry. Before I start painting, I moisten the colours and use them in the same consistency as if they were freshly squeezed out of the tube. Because only a thin layer at the top is wet, I feel free to pollute one colour with another while I paint and mix back and forth. To have lots of pure pigment available at any time, all I do is wipe off the thin contaminated layer from the top of the colour and there is the clean paint waiting to be used.

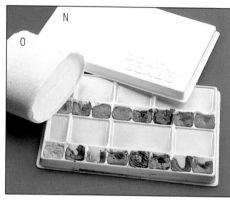

I also make a moisture-controlling contraption out of a roll of toilet paper. I take out the centre core, flatten the roll, and wrap a few sheets of lint-free paper towel round the outside (folded to the same width as the paper roll). I then tape its edge to stop it from unrolling. The toilet paper is very absorbent but it breaks down quickly when it is moistened, releasing tiny particles that can be carried onto the painting by the brushes. The wet-strength paper towel around the roll prevents this from happening. The absorbency is still there but the surface will not break down even in heavy use. Because the brushes usually absorb too much water when they are dipped into a bucket, I make a habit of touching my brush to the paper roll's surface before I dip into the colour.

Controlling moisture in the washes begins by controlling it in the brush.

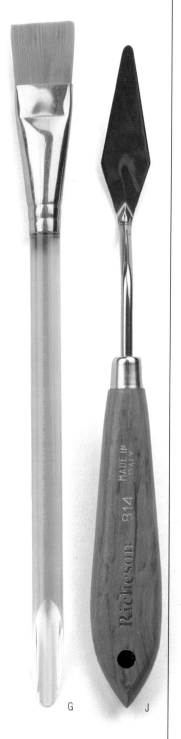

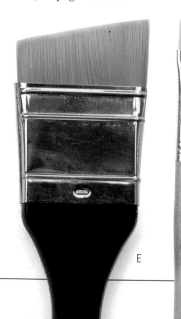

CHAPTER 1

Qualities of Transparent Watercolour Pigments

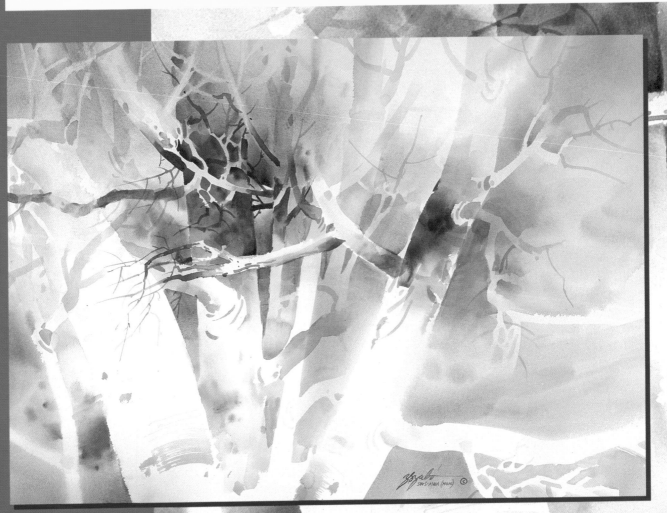

Emerald Tree
48x71cm (19x28in)
Collection of Gianni Maimeri.

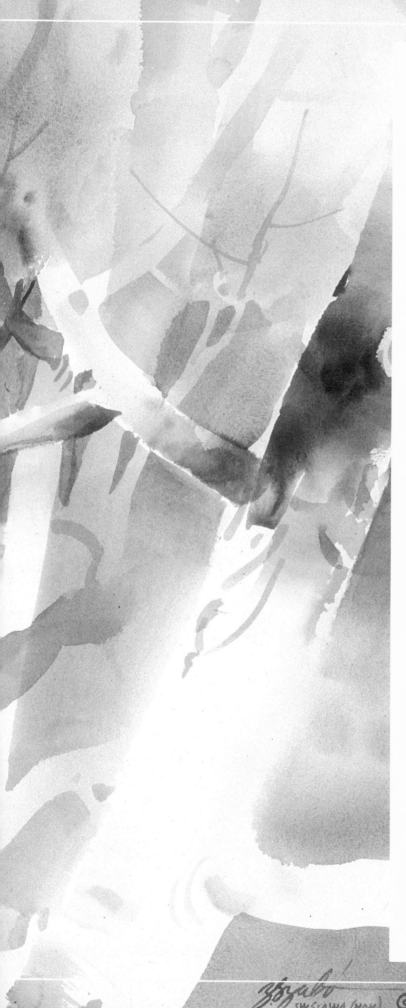

Artists, being creatures of curiosity, will make changes in their palettes during a lifetime of painting, but whatever palette you start off with must be based on a thorough knowledge of each and every colour. This knowledge should include the complete nature and built-in qualities of the colours.

Like most watercolourists, I spent several decades of my career using Winsor & Newton watercolours almost exclusively. But the popularity of these wonderful colours did not deter me from experimenting with other brands. I feel that I know the nature of most Winsor & Newton pigments, particularly those I kept on my palette, as intimately as anyone can. As the years went by, however, I found it more and more inconvenient to stick stubbornly with the same colours, particularly if they were not completely permanent. Even though the company is very good about declaring the level of permanence of their pigments, I decided to test some other major brands such as Grumbacher, Rowney, Lukas, Holbein, Da Vinci, Sennelier, Blockx and most recently, Maimeri. Winsor & Newton had the edge over some of the other manufacturers until recently, but they all have some unique quality typical to each brand.

Because I refer to generic colour names throughout this book, you would be wise to test your own favourite brands and colours to identify their peculiarities. Remember that the nature of colours – even if they are called by the same name – may vary from one brand to another.

On the following pages are samples of watercolour paints that I've categorized according to some important characteristics, such as transparency and opacity, staining and non-staining, reflective and sedimentary, etc. But be aware that some of the colours' behaviour will vary from one brand of *paper* to another. Expect consistency of paint behaviour only on good quality, all-rag paper.

Transparent Colours

These wonderful, glowing, luminous colours that all watercolourists love behave similarly to stained glass. They let light penetrate through the wash and reflect from the paper through the colour. These are the most suitable colours for glazing (applying a wet wash over a completely dry wash without disturbing the lower layer) because they don't build up when they overlap. These true transparent colours make the most glowing, clear darks, but some of these pigments are very strong and tend to dominate when they are mixed with other colours.

If you want to use only true transparent colours, you could use liquid watercolours. Unfortunately, most of the watercolours in liquid form are not very permanent, so you need to research their lightfastness. However, even if you find a permanent liquid watercolour brand, you'd still rob yourself of the opportunity to use the excitingly varied nature of your pigments. My advice is to use an artist's quality transparent watercolour in the tube, made by a reputable company.

Transparent Colours include:

- Phthalo violet
- Phthalo blue
- Phthalo green
- Scarlet lake
- Rose madder
- New gamboge
- Hooker's green
- Cyanine blue
- Indian yellow

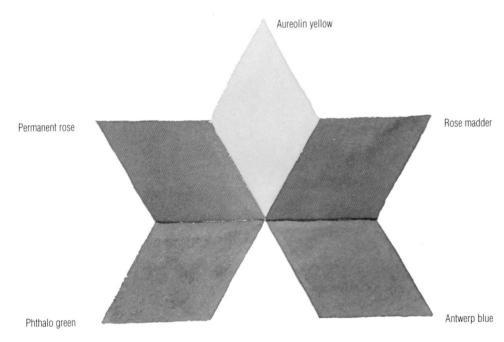

Aureolin yellow

Permanent rose

Rose madder

Phthalo green

Antwerp blue

Phthalo violet · Phthalo blue · Phthalo green · Scarlet lake · Rose madder · Permanent rose · New gamboge · Hooker's green · Cyanine blue · Indian yellow

Testing Transparency

To test the transparency level of a colour, draw a 6mm (¼in) thick line with a black waterproof marker or with Indian ink. Over this line, place a brush stroke of the desired colours in medium dark consistency. Transparent colours will not show at all where they cross over the black line because the black absorbs all the light.

Opaque Colours

Though all watercolours called transparent are luminous in thin washes, some have more body than others. These opaque or body colours are capable of covering other dry washes when they are applied in a thick consistency, even if the dry underwash is dark and the top colour is light. They are not truly opaque, as acrylics are, but are more so than the transparent colours.

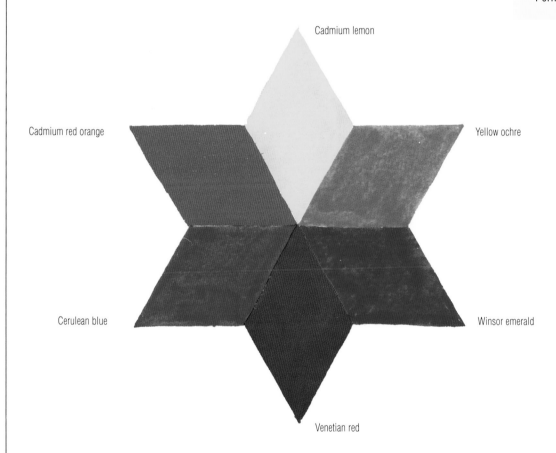

Cadmium lemon

Cadmium red orange

Yellow ochre

Cerulean blue

Winsor emerald

Venetian red

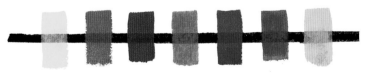

Cadmium yellow · Cadmium red-orange · Venetian red · Yellow ochre · Winsor emerald · Cerulean blue · Naples yellow

Testing Opacity

To test the degree of opacity in a colour, first draw a 6mm (¼in) wide line with a black waterproof marker or Indian ink. Over this line, place a medium-dark brush stroke of the desired colour. The degree by which the colour covers up the black line indicates how opaque it is.

Reflective Colours

Reflective colours behave the opposite way to the true transparent pigments. The most transparent colours act like stained glass. They let the light penetrate through the wash and reflect from the paper through the colour. Reflective colours let a certain amount of light get through to the surface of the white paper, but they are also capable of reflecting light from the *surface of the paint*.

If painted over a waterproof black line, reflective colours look very transparent while wet, but show a little of their own hue after they dry. Opaque, semi-opaque and reflective colours don't glaze well because they build up to a thick layer. All opaque colours that are light in hue are reflective, but not all reflective colours are opaque. A few reflective colours are considered transparent, yet they reflect light when they are applied in heavy consistency.

Reflective Colours include:

- Cobalt violet
- Cobalt blue
- Raw sienna
- Raw umber
- Viridian green
- Aureolin yellow
- Magenta
- Cobalt green

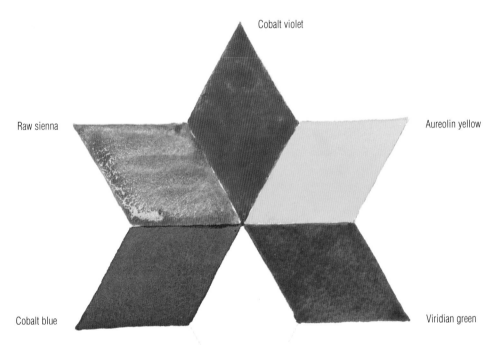

Cobalt violet — Aureolin yellow — Raw sienna — Cobalt blue — Viridian green

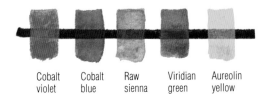

Cobalt violet | Cobalt blue | Raw sienna | Viridian green | Aureolin yellow

Testing Reflectiveness

The test for reflective colours is the same as for the opaque colours (see page 17).

Sedimentary Colours

Sedimentary, or granulating, colours are made from physically heavy pigments. Because of their weight, sedimentary colours sink in the water like pebbles. On rough or cold-pressed paper, they are first to land in the low, hollow spots of the paper. On the smooth surface of hot-pressed paper, they settle quickly, but water rivulets create little river-like separations. All this behaviour translates graphically into texture. A sandpaper-like grain is the nature of these pigments. When you mix them in a wet wash with other colours, they will look grainy and may separate, while transparent colours will dissolve in water like tea and stay active as long as the wash is wet. When sedimentary and non-sedimentary colours are mixed, each colour is individually visible, for example, manganese blue and burnt sienna, and raw sienna and phthalo blue.

Sedimentary Colours include:
- Ultramarine blue
- Raw sienna
- Raw umber
- Sepia
- Cobalt violet
- Viridian green
- Manganese blue

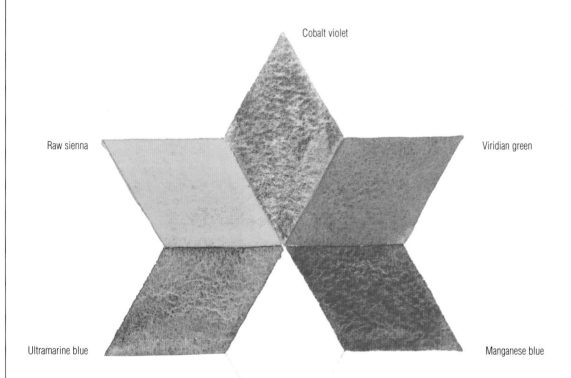

Cobalt violet

Raw sienna

Viridian green

Ultramarine blue

Manganese blue

No Testing Necessary

There's no need to test sedimentary colours. Their grainy texture is easy to see, particularly if the colours is applied with lots of water in the brush.

Staining Colours

Dark Staining

When a pigment tints the fibre of the paper it is called a staining colour. These colours behave like a dye. The staining nature of a pigment is not relevant to other qualities. Opaque, sedimentary or transparent colours can be either staining or nonstaining. The degree of staining quality of a pigment is important to know only if you intend to lift out a colour. A staining colour will show a tint of its hue even after you have tried to wet-scrub and blot off the paint. This behaviour remains even if the staining colour is mixed with other nonstaining colours.

Light Staining

These few pigments stain a little if they are applied with heavy pressure or with a scrubbing technique. However, their hue retains only a light tint in the paper. If they are mixed with other nonstaining or light staining colours, the resulting mix will stain according to the strength of the dominant colour.

Dark Staining Colours include:

- All phthalo colours
- Burnt sienna
- Scarlet lake
- Sap green
- Hooker's green

Light Staining Colours include:

- Gold ochre
- Cobalt blue
- Gamboge yellow
- Cerulean blue
- Magenta

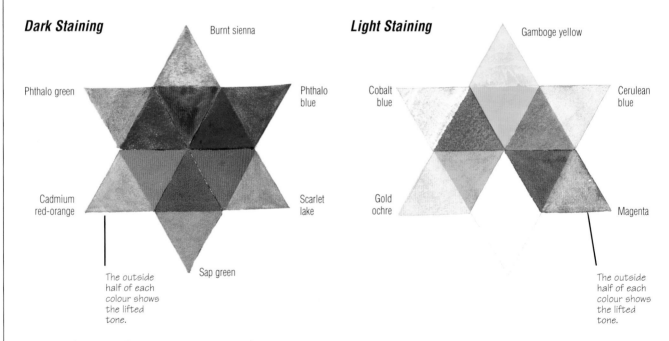

Dark Staining

Burnt sienna

Phthalo green

Phthalo blue

Cadmium red-orange

Scarlet lake

Sap green

The outside half of each colour shows the lifted tone.

Light Staining

Gamboge yellow

Cobalt blue

Cerulean blue

Gold ochre

Magenta

The outside half of each colour shows the lifted tone.

Testing Staining Strength

To test the staining strength of a colour, paint a rich brush stroke and let it dry. After loosening the pigment with a very wet brush (such as a small oil-painting brush), blot it off with a tissue. A staining colour will get a little lighter but will leave a strong impression of its hue in the fibre of the paper. It's important to test on the same kind of paper as you will use for your painting. The staining quality of a colour may vary from one brand of paper to another.

Nonstaining Colours

These colours cannot stain at all. They are ideally suited for lifting out because on some papers (Arches, for example), you can recover pure white paper if you remove the wet or dry colours by scrubbing with a wet brush. On some papers a slight residue will remain that shows against white paper, but will look white when surrounded with darker painted shapes. These colours do not penetrate the fibre of the paper, but just sit on top of it, held in place only by the sticking strength of the binding agent in the paint.

Nonstaining Colours include:
- Emerald green
- Permanent rose
- Manganese blue
- Aureolin yellow
- Cobalt violet

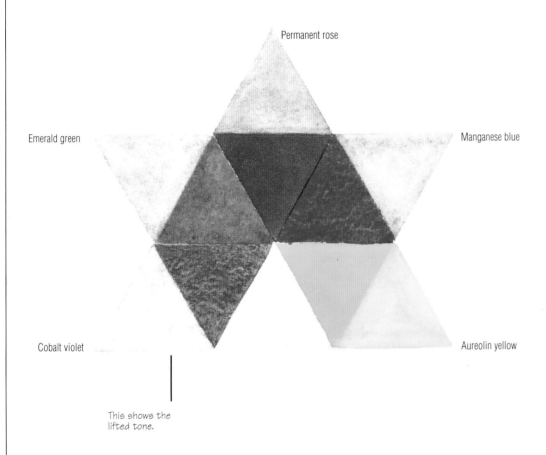

Permanent rose

Emerald green

Manganese blue

Cobalt violet

Aureolin yellow

This shows the lifted tone.

Testing Nonstaining Colours

Test a nonstaining colour by painting a brush stroke in a medium-dark tone and letting it dry. With a well moistened scrubbing brush, loosen the colours and blot it off with a tissue. A nonstaining colour will come off completely and white paper will be recovered. Because paper brands react differently, test with the same kind of paper as you will use for your painting. This colour star was painted on 300g/m² (140lb) Waterford cold-pressed paper.

Dominance

Extra attention should be paid to this most often overlooked colour peculiarity. Colour dominance needs to be considered when more than one colour is mixed into a wash. The same colour combination may result in an almost infinite variety of colours depending on the proportions of the mix. Whichever pigment is the most *dominant* in the mix will impose its characteristics on the wash, not only in the hue but in all other aspects of its nature as well, such as staining or nonstaining, opaque or transparent.

If the dominant colour is manganese blue (a sedimentary pigment) and the secondary colour is burnt sienna (a transparent colour), the mixed colour will not only be a bluer hue but will also be a grainy-textured colour and will lift off better than burnt sienna would lift off by itself. This is because manganese blue is the dominant colour and not only its hue but also its other natural characteristics impose their dominance over the other colour.

If you intend to dominate a wash with a gentle colour (permanent rose) and use a basically strong colour (phthalo green) as a weaker complement, as in the example at top right, you must increase the amount of the dominant colour (permanent rose) in the mix and substantially reduce the quantity of the secondary pigment (phthalo green). However, when the dominant colour is strong (phthalo green) and the secondary is moderate (permanent rose), naturally the quantity of the colours in the mix reverses.

Staining Dominance

Whenever you use a staining colour by itself, it tints the fibres of the paper and cannot be removed completely. When staining colours are mixed with other weaker hues (but are still dominant in the mix), they can still leave their hue in the paper, though to a lesser extent.

The most obvious influence of staining dominance shows up when you try to lift off the colour after it has dried. Whichever staining colour touches the paper will dominate the lifted colour, regardless of what other colours may be glazed on top of it. If the staining colours are applied together in one wash, the lifted colour will favour the dominant hue. If neither dominates, the combined colour will appear in a lighter tone. Here, below right, I used two very strong staining colours, alizarin crimson and phthalo green. Below the two squares I made a dark wash of equal amounts of both colours.

To the right of the two colours I painted a colour bar with alizarin crimson and let it dry (I left a little of it showing). I glazed an estimated equal tone of phthalo green on top of it and again allowed it to dry.

Next, I did the same thing but in reverse order, with phthalo green first, then alizarin crimson on top.

After letting them dry, I rinsed loose as much of the combined colours as I could with a small soft brush loaded with water, and blotted it off with a paper tissue. The soft lifted-out area ended up light grey on the lower colour bar, pink on the first colour bar and green on the second.

Dominance

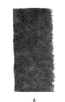
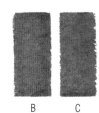

Permanent rose   Phthalo green   A   B   C

A Permanent rose + phthalo green mixed in equal amounts

B Same mix but with more permanent rose, less phthalo green

C Same two colours, but stronger phthalo green

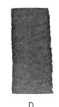

Permanent rose   Phthalo green   Gamboge yellow   D   E   F   G

D Permanent rose, phthalo green, gamboge yellow in equal amounts

E Permanent rose dominates

F Phthalo green dominates

G Gamboge yellow dominates

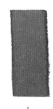

Permanent rose   Phthalo green   Gamboge yellow   Cyanine blue   H   I   J   K   L

H Same three colours plus cyanine blue in equal amounts

I Permanent rose dominates

J Phthalo green dominates

K Gamboge yellow dominates

L Cyanine blue dominates

Staining Dominance

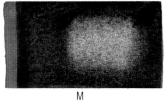
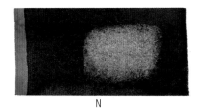

Alizarin crimson   Phthalo green   M   N

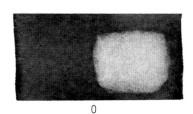

O

M Alizarin crimson painted first, with phthalo green glazed on top

N Phthalo green painted first, with alizarin crimson glazed on top

O A mix of equal amounts of alizarin crimson and phthalo green

Palettes

Maimeri watercolours make up my newest and favourite palette. They relate to Nature's colour spectrum because of the pure and glowing colours. Whenever I want to paint happy and colourful subjects I use Maimeri colours. They are just a little bit more intense and luminous and they seem to hold their chroma very well after drying. I lay them out on my palette in an order similar to the colour wheel.

My next two favourite palettes are made up of Blockx watercolours, and Winsor & Newton. The selected palettes shown opposite resemble each other closely. The manufacturers offer a lot more colours that I don't consider essential for my way of painting with watercolour; I selected each one of these palettes based on my own needs. Though they are not duplicates, they are as close as their natures permit, considering the differences between the two brands. You might say these are my two interchangeable duplicate palettes. They include colours that are essential for my special techniques, such as Winsor & Newton sepia, either brand's manganese, Blockx magenta and Blockx green.

My Maimeri palette (Italian extremely permanent colours):

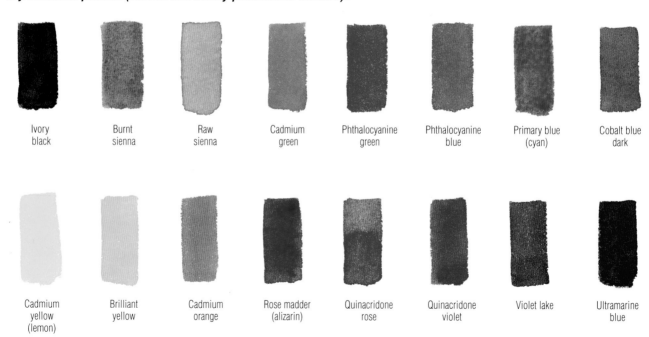

| Ivory black | Burnt sienna | Raw sienna | Cadmium green | Phthalocyanine green | Phthalocyanine blue | Primary blue (cyan) | Cobalt blue dark |
| Cadmium yellow (lemon) | Brilliant yellow | Cadmium orange | Rose madder (alizarin) | Quinacridone rose | Quinacridone violet | Violet lake | Ultramarine blue |

My Blockx palette (Belgian extremely permanent colours):

Gamboge
yellow

Gold
ochre

Burnt sienna
light

Rose
madder

Magenta

Vandyke
brown

Ultramarine blue
deep

Manganese
blue

Aureolin
yellow

Cobalt
violet

Cadmium
red-orange

Cobalt blue

Emerald
green

Blockx green
(phthalo)

Cyanine
blue

Cerulean
blue

My Winsor & Newton palette (British permanent colours):

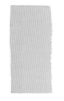
New gamboge
yellow

Raw
sienna

Burnt
sienna

Permanent
rose

Sepia

Antwerp blue

French
ultramarine

Manganese
blue

Aureolin
yellow

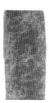
Cobalt
violet

Scarlet
lake

Viridian
green

Winsor
green

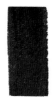
Winsor
blue

Cobalt
blue

Cerulean
blue

CHAPTER 2

Rules of Reflection

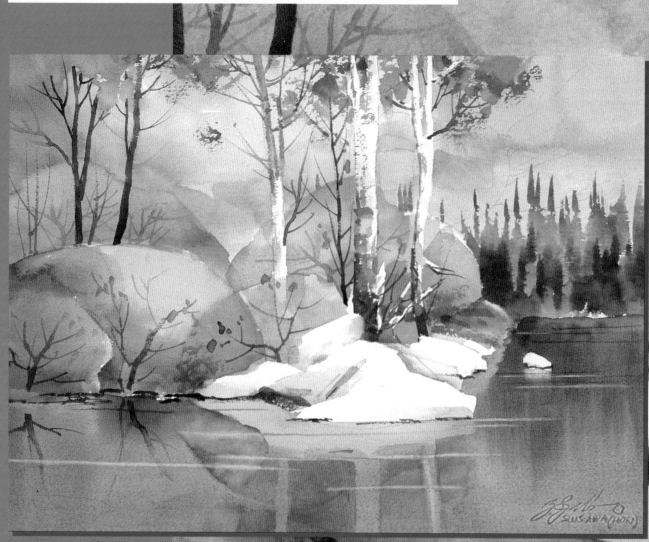

Pearly Whites
27.5x37cm (11x14½in)

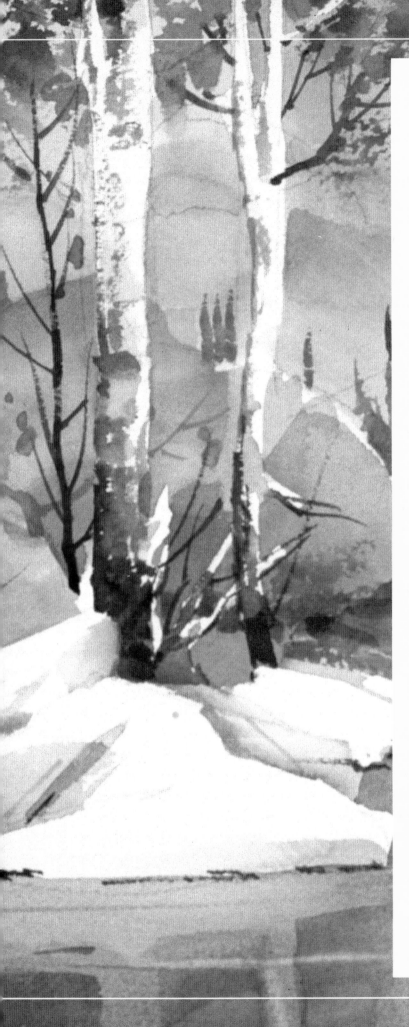

The Rules of Reflection

It may surprise you that even some well established artists do not know much about the rules of reflection. Through my years of teaching I have found reflections to be extremely troublesome to my students, in spite of the fact that water is one of their favourite subjects. Rules sound so serious and scientific. The creative mind wants to turn them off or avoid the whole subject, but this robs the artist of the rewards of succeeding with reflecting subjects.

Perfect and Imperfect Reflectors

Because reflection is controlled by the laws of physics, which are absolute, you don't have to worry about exceptions. Reflecting surfaces may be broken down into two categories: perfect and imperfect reflectors. Perfect reflecting surfaces do not have local colour of their own; imperfect ones do. For our purposes a mirror is a perfect reflector but water is not.

A Reflector's Local Colour

To identify the local colour of a translucent liquid with a reflective surface such as water, you must first eliminate the reflection. Let's take a hypothetical situation. You are in a boat on a lake. If you lean over the edge, where your head blocks out the sky's reflection, the local colour appears. We call this the water's own local colour (without any reflection). If the water is very shallow, its bottom will show through as the local colour. In the case of a large body of water, the mass volume of the water combined with all its minerals and microscopic life will compose the local colour.

On the following pages you will see how easy it is to understand the rules of reflection. I have included not only small painted illustrations, but also a lot of untouched photographs. I hope that the camera will convince even the most determined doubting Thomas. Now let's look at some rules of reflection depicted by the most common reflective surface: water.

RULE 1

Any given point on an object must reflect directly below itself.

This rule is true whether the object stands straight or leans to the side. For example, if an object stands upright its reflection will continue straight down. If an object leans to the left, its reflection will also lean to the left so that all points on it, including its far tip, will reflect directly below themselves. If the object leans to the right, its reflection will also tilt to the right.

Left- or right-tilting reflections appear in exactly the same angle as their corresponding objects and cannot be shorter or longer. They must be the same length so that the far tip of the object reflects below itself.

The palm trees reflecting in the still water stand at a near-perfect vertical. Therefore the reflection of each tree continues straight down from the trunk of the tree. The reflection of the leafy top of each tree is directly below the leafy top of the tree itself. The distance from the bottom of the tree to the top in the reflection is exactly equal to the height of the real tree, even though part of the trunk is not visible in the reflection.

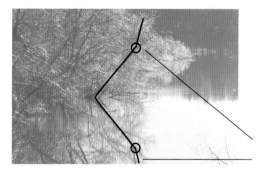

Vertical object
Height of tree
Eye level
Height of reflection
Vertical reflection

In this photo the dark branches are leaning to the right. So are the reflections. In fact, each point on each branch reflects exactly below itself. Try to pair up a spot on the centre branch with its reflection. The easiest place to pinpoint is the bend in the branch. Directly below it you'll find the reflection bending to the same side at the same angle.

Bend in branch

Matching bend in reflection

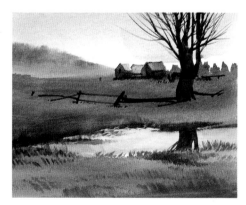

In this painting, the puddle of water is the only reflective surface. If the puddle reached all the way to the tree, it would reflect the tree from the roots up. But the puddle is located so that only a portion of the trunk is reflected.

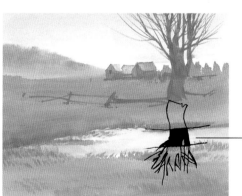

Reflected portion

To determine what part of an object would reflect in a puddle, use this simple trick. Trace the object on tracing paper. Turn the tracing paper over just below the object. On your painting, trace the portion of the object that falls on the puddle.

RULE 2

An object tilting towards you will foreshorten and will seem shorter than its reflection.

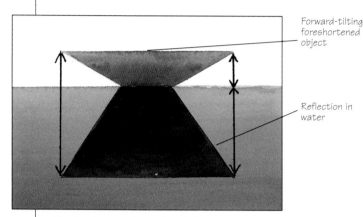

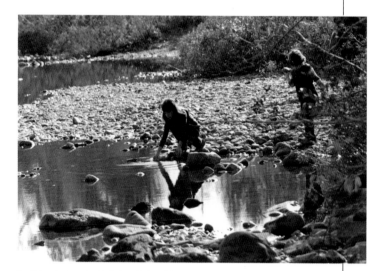

The top (magenta) portion of this illustration leans towards you and is severely foreshortened. The black shape represents its reflection in the green water and appears longer than the tilted object. The more severe the tilt, the greater the difference.

In this photo, the height of the child leaning towards the viewer is shorter than her reflection in the water.

RULE 3

When an object tilts away from you, its reflection becomes shorter than the object itself.

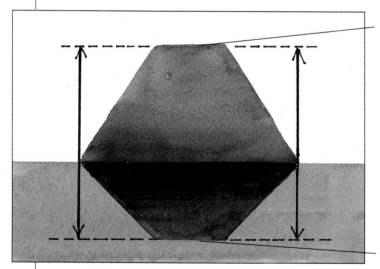

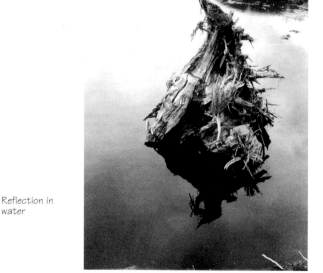

Imagine that the magenta shape is leaning away from you. Because of perspective, the reflection (black) will appear foreshortened. The situation is exactly the reverse of the diagram in Rule 2, above.

Because this tree stump is leaning away from the viewer, its reflection appears shorter.

RULE 4

The reflection of an object appears the way you would see it if your eyes were on the surface of the water, where the reflection is located.

Your vantage point is always higher than the reflection on the water's surface. This is the reason why you may see the inside of a small boat on the water, but its reflection will show only the outside of the boat's hull.

The underside of an object leaning towards you, such as a branch, may not be visible from your vantage point. However, its *reflection* will show the underside because it is presented to the reflecting surface of the water.

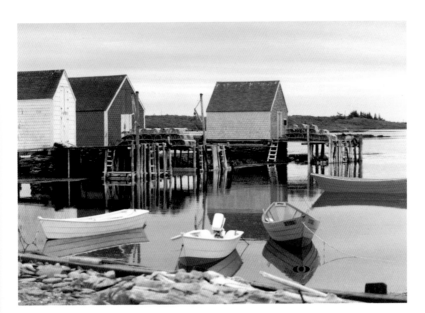

In this photograph you can see the inside of the boats, but the reflections show only their hulls. However, if your eyes were on the water where the reflections are, you would then see exactly what the reflections show. Viewed from the surface of the water, the hulls would hide the boats' interiors.

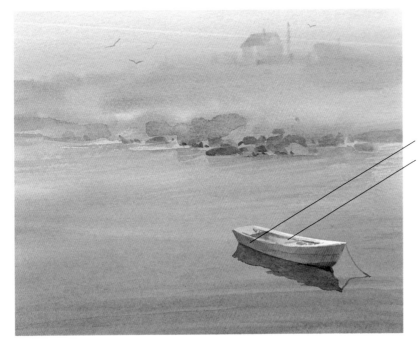

The area that is reflected.

What you can see in addition to the side.

This small watercolour is a painted example to illustrate this rule. The reflection shows only the boat's hull, not the interior details.

RULE 5

The tone of a reflection is controlled by the darkest tone of the water's local colour.

No reflection can be any darker than the water's local colour, regardless of how dark the originating object may be.

- If the tone of the reflecting object is lighter than the darkest tone of the water's local colour, they will combine and the reflection will be darker than the object.
- If the object has the same tone as the local colour of the water, its reflection will also have the same tone.
- If the object is darker than the water's local colour, it still reflects the same as the local colour.
- In milky water the darkest tone of the local colour is relatively light.

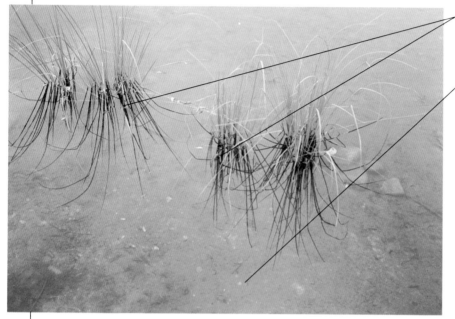

Reflection of weeds blocks out the sky and shows true value of local colour.

Colour and tone of reflected sky and the muddy bottom combined.

Here, the colour of most of the water's surface is a combination of the shallow bottom (local colour) and the sky's reflection. The colour of the fresh green weeds is very close in tone to this tone. Where the weeds block out the sky's reflection, the dark, muddy bottom dominates the colour and of the weeds' reflections.

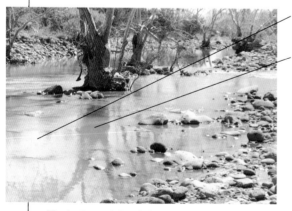

Sky's reflection plus mud combined.

Sky's reflection is blocked out by the tree trunk. Reflection shows only the deepest tone of the local colour.

The bottom of the shallow creek (the local colour) in this photo is light. Consequently the reflection of the dark tree is lighter than the tree trunk itself.

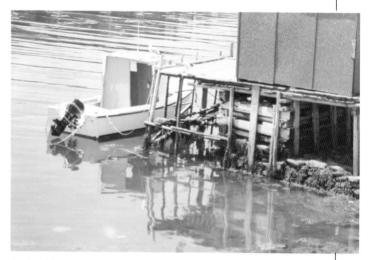

As the tide came in, it churned up the particles in the water and made the water milky, causing the dark shapes to reflect lighter than their own tone. In fact, they reflect exactly the same tone as the deepest tone of the water's local colour, a mid-tone grey.

The colour of a reflection is influenced by the local colour of the water.

A white boat will reflect a little darker than its own tone but in the same *colour* as the water itself. The reflection of a neutral colour will be dominated by the local colour of the water. Bright colours combine with the colour of the water. For example, orange colour in grey water will reflect as a greyed orange.

Because still water resembles glass, water reflections may be imitated on a sheet of glass for study purposes. You can place white, black or coloured paper under the glass to change its local colour as well as its reflective quality.

Whites reflect darker than their own tone and show the local colour of the water (blue-grey).

Tan wall reflects bluer because it combines with the local colour of the water.

Blue boat reflects darker blue-grey.

Orange pole reflects greyer because it combines with the water's local colour.

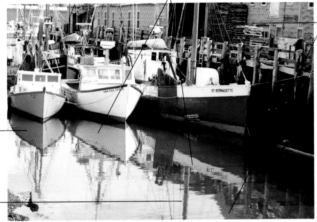

The colours of the reflections show the objects' own colours combined with the water's local colour (blue-grey). Notice how the white hull reflects darker than its own tone and shows a blue-grey colour. This identifies the water's hue.

Reflections of neutral colours are dominated by the water's local colour.

Bright red colour combines with the local colour and reflects reddish-brown.

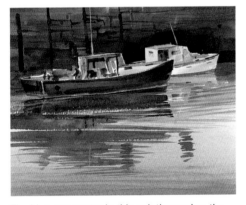

The blue-grey water in this painting makes the yellow-green boat (as well as the white one) reflect bluer. The orange raincoat shows its own colour combined with the water's hue.

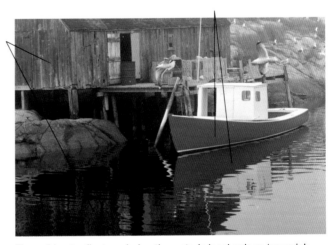

The red boat reflects red plus the water's local colour (greenish brown), resulting in a reddish brown. All the other colours are neutral enough that their reflections are totally dominated by the brownish local colour of the water.

RULE 7

The angle of incidence and the angle of reflection are always the same and they are inseparable.

This rule is very important because it determines what objects reflect where and why. It can be very useful to you, especially when painting in the studio, to figure out the correct placement of a reflection.

Though still true, it is more difficult to see this rule in action on moving water. The movement of waves makes it difficult to concentrate on the reflection. In addition, because the reflecting surface of a wave is not horizontal like still water, its slant can cause some confusion. The angle of incidence and the angle of reflection relate to a tilted surface, not to a flat surface.

To help you understand this rule as it applies to waves, experiment with a small hand mirror. When the mirror lies flat on the table it reflects one view. If you pick up one edge of the mirror so that it is at an angle to the table, it will reflect a different view.

Still Water

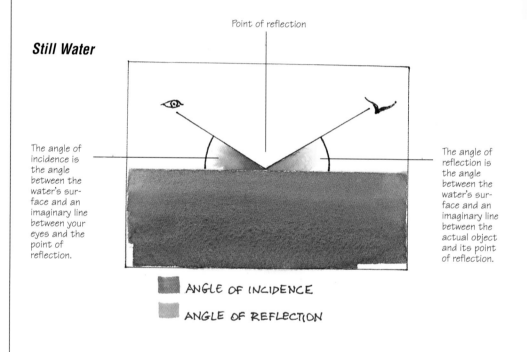

Point of reflection

The angle of incidence is the angle between the water's surface and an imaginary line between your eyes and the point of reflection.

The angle of reflection is the angle between the water's surface and an imaginary line between the actual object and its point of reflection.

■ ANGLE OF INCIDENCE

■ ANGLE OF REFLECTION

Wavy Water

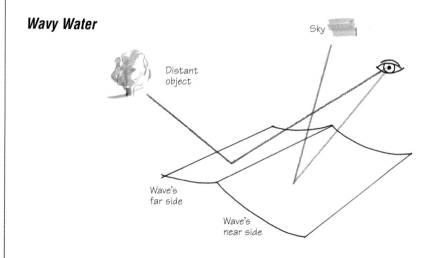

Sky

Distant object

Wave's far side

Wave's near side

When there are waves present, the angle of reflection bounces off a *tilted* surface rather than a flat one. As you can see, the angle is different on the far side of the wave to that on the near side. This causes the eye to see a different image in each side of the wave.

Characteristics of Waves

Moving water can be broken down into its components, called waves. Moving waves are difficult to study, but a photograph will show them in detail. Waves have near and far sides. The near sides of the waves appear wide and they are slanted on a steep angle. Because they tilt slightly away from you, they often reflect the high sky combined with the water's local colour. The local colour affects the hue of the wave's near side because the steep angle allows you to look partly into the body of the wave.

The wave's far side appears narrower because of foreshortening. The angle of incidence and the angle of reflection are low as they bounce off the wave's far side. Consequently it will reflect the low, distant sky and whatever else is in the visual path of the angle of reflection. Because of the severe tilt, the wave displays only reflection and does not show any local colour.

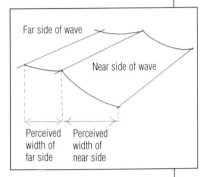

In this diagram the far side of the wave appears to be narrower than the near side because of foreshortening.

When the background is dark, its reflection in the far side of the waves looks darker than the near side's tone.

Far sides of waves reflect the bright white side of the building.

Near sides of waves are medium tone and wider than far sides. They look darker against the light-reflecting background.

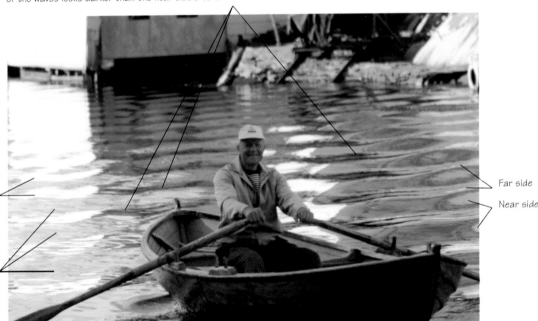

Far side

Near side

You can learn many things about waves from this photograph:
- You can see that the nearer sides of the waves appear wider than the far sides.
- There are four main tones affecting the colour of the water. From lightest to darkest they are: the white (left) side of the building, the blue sky, the local colour of the water, and the dark side of the building.
- The wide (near) sides of the waves reflect mostly what's above; the narrow (far) sides of the waves reflect mostly what's behind.

RULE 8

Reflections are not in *the water but* on *its surface.*

When a reflection stretches across and reaches the water near you, it follows the movement of the nearby ripples. An image reflecting on moving water will wiggle on the dancing waves. Waves have perspective like railway sleepers. Wiggly waves close to the reflecting object will appear smaller than those close to you because of perspective. Also, the reflection of the far tip of the object in the nearer waves will start to skip just before it stops reflecting on the waves' near sides. For a short space it keeps reflecting only on their far sides. Finally, the whole waves reflect only the sky.

    The reason for this is that the high *angles of reflection* bouncing off the near sides of the waves will be the first to pass over the top of the image and stop reflecting it. However, from the far sides of the same waves the *angles of reflection* still meet the object and must reflect. Their angles of reflection are low enough to allow the top of the image to reflect a little longer than it does on the near sides.

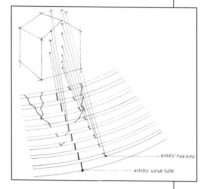

Note how many more angles of reflection hit the building from the flatter far sides of the waves than from the steeper near sides.

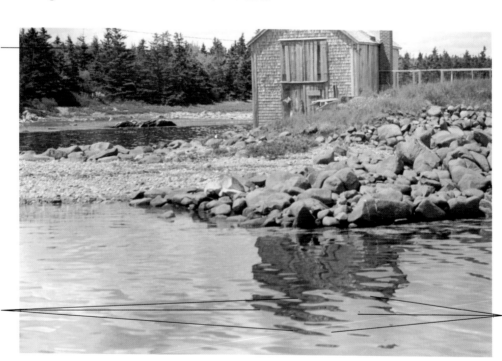

The trees are too far away to reflect in the foreground water.

The far sides of the foreground waves still show the reflection of the building.

The near sides of these same foreground waves reflect only the sky.

This old fishing hut is reflecting into very wavy water. You can study how the top of the building skips the near sides of the closer waves first, while it still shows its reflection in the far sides of the same waves.

If a gentle wind blows from the side, making many tiny waves, you may see breeze patterns on the water's surface.

These light, zigzagging shapes often interrupt an otherwise perfectly calm reflection. They are dominated by the colour and tone of the sky. Because these shapes have a habit of disappearing, you need to freeze them in your mind and design their shapes to suit your composition.

This breeze shape, reflecting the colour of the sky, looks confusing at this location. I would leave it out of my painting.

This useful breeze shape sets off the sandbars.

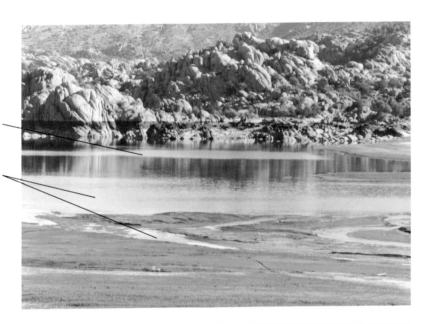

Calm Water
In this photo I managed to freeze the dancing action of the breeze as it was breaking up the motionless surface. The blue colour is the reflection of the sky. The light tone of the sky supplied a very pleasant contrast to the sandbars in front.

Choppy Water
When a stronger wind causes the water to be choppy, the sideways-rolling, choppy waves reflect only the sky colour. The objects above the water, such as the boat, do not reflect.

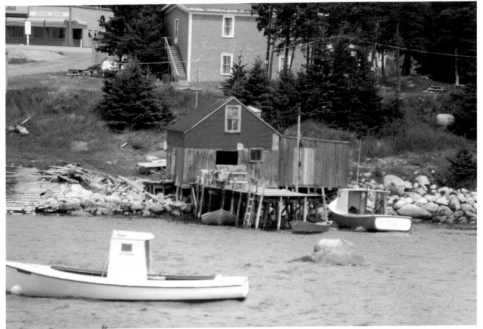

RULE 10

When a very light subject against a very dark background reflects in gently moving water, its reflection may appear much longer than the length of the object itself.

The brighter the image and the darker the background, the greater the contrast will be. Strong contrast causes the reflection to stretch farther. The strongest contrast and longest reflection possible is usually caused by the light source itself (such as low sun, moon, electric light at night). This reflection phenomenon is caused by the fact that the water's local colour is very dark. The dark secondary light source (for example, a late sky) cannot illuminate the particles in the water that form the water's local colour. (During daylight the whole sky releases light and brightens the body of water.) The delicately moving waves pick up the only bright reflection on varying spots of their shiny surface without any competition from neighboring mid-tones. However, the light reflection will reduce in intensity as it travels farther from its origin and closer to you. The farther the reflection is located from the subject, the more the local colour absorbs its tone until it consumes it.

If there are some very dim mid-tones surrounding the bright object, the length of the reflection will be moderately long. However, if the background is black, the reflection may reach the near edge of the visible surface of the water.

If the water is not moving, the reflecting bright object will be the same size as it appears in reality, even if the subject is a high-contrast light source.

The bright sun reflects only on the far sides of the waves and continues to the bottom of the photo.

The brightest object is the light source.

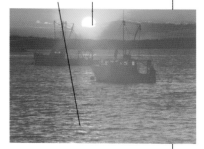

The sun, the light source on this photo, shows an extremely strong contrast. Even though the water is very choppy, its reflection dances all the way down to the closest waves.

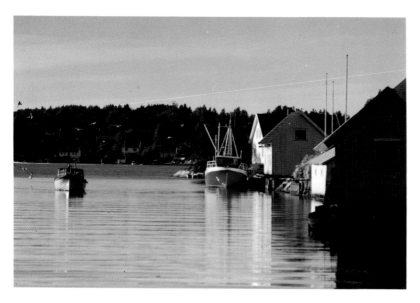

The red boat and the white walls of the buildings that face the setting sun are brightly lit. The contrasting tones of the lightest and darkest shapes stretch down to the bottom of the photograph, farther than the actual height of the shapes.

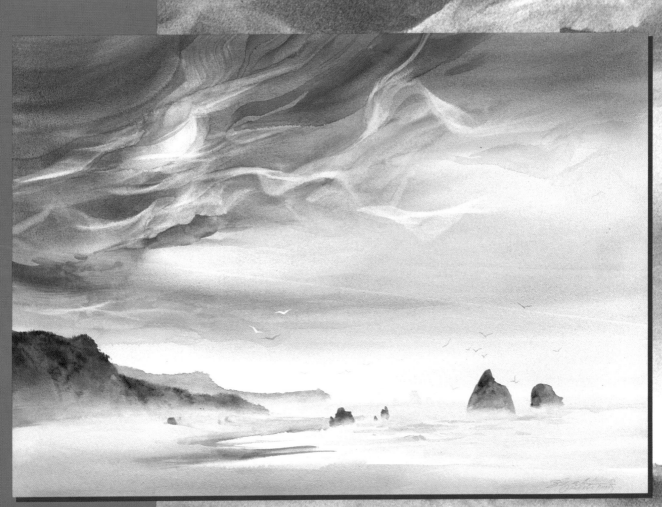

CHAPTER 3

Composition and Design

Smoke Storm
48x71cm (19x28in)
Collection of Willa McNeill.

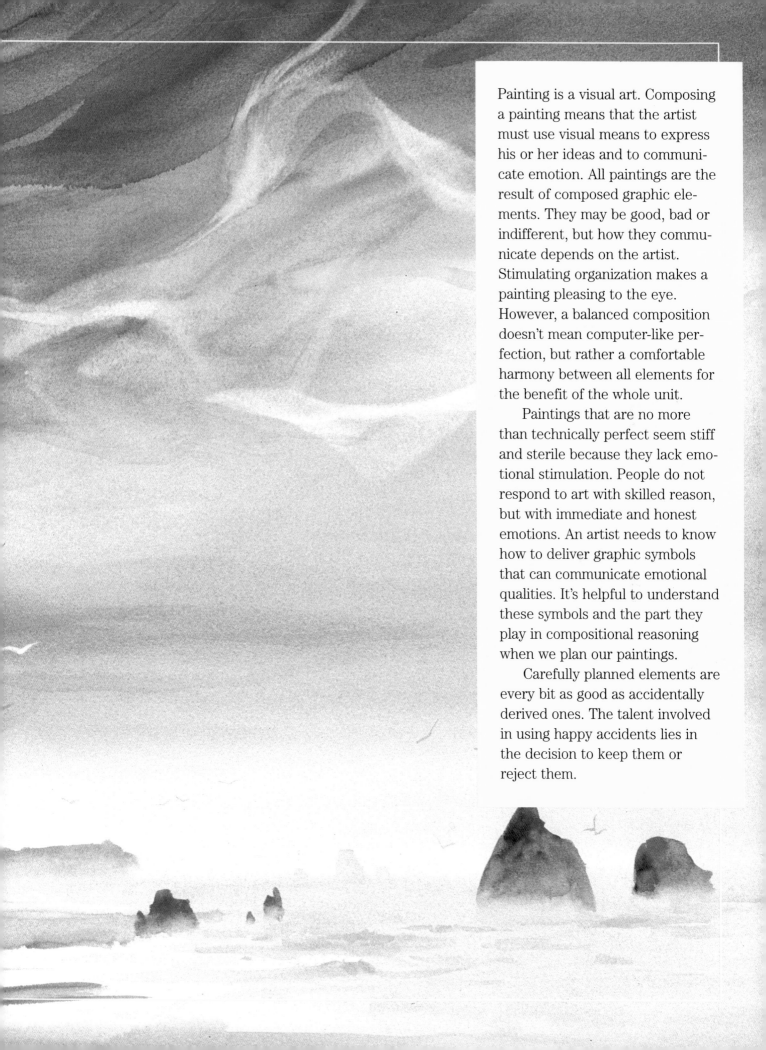

Painting is a visual art. Composing a painting means that the artist must use visual means to express his or her ideas and to communicate emotion. All paintings are the result of composed graphic elements. They may be good, bad or indifferent, but how they communicate depends on the artist. Stimulating organization makes a painting pleasing to the eye. However, a balanced composition doesn't mean computer-like perfection, but rather a comfortable harmony between all elements for the benefit of the whole unit.

Paintings that are no more than technically perfect seem stiff and sterile because they lack emotional stimulation. People do not respond to art with skilled reason, but with immediate and honest emotions. An artist needs to know how to deliver graphic symbols that can communicate emotional qualities. It's helpful to understand these symbols and the part they play in compositional reasoning when we plan our paintings.

Carefully planned elements are every bit as good as accidentally derived ones. The talent involved in using happy accidents lies in the decision to keep them or reject them.

The Illusion of Space

A good painting is a successful illusion indicating more than a flat, two-dimensional surface. The job of an artist is to achieve a desired new reality including the possible illusion of three dimensions.

The first step is to choose the size and proportions of the watercolour paper. This is called the support shape because it will support all the details of the painting. This two-dimensional shape represents potential three-dimensional space hosting elements that have depth in reality. Moreover the illusion of depth in the painting must be convincing enough to trick our eyes into seeing three dimensions.

Of course, these hints apply mostly to representational work. Non-objective design allows for unlimited distortions of scale, but a painting based on visual reality needs to meet the requirements of depth and scale.

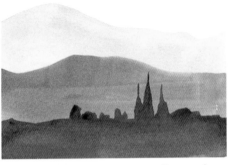

Distant objects appear smaller, paler, cooler (bluer) and less defined than close ones.
The way children and primitive artists like to place distant elements above closer ones is an instinctive attempt to imply the illusion of depth.

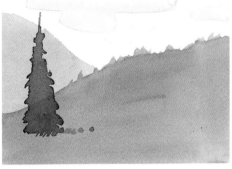

Overlapping objects add depth.
When a shape overlaps another, it will appear to be in front of the one it partly covers.

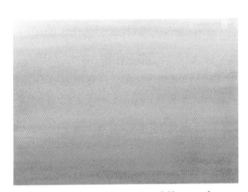

Warm colours advance while cool hues recede.
Perspective allows the shapes within a painting to appear as if they were located in three-dimensional space. Colour perspective allows objects to appear as if they exist in an atmosphere that has depth.

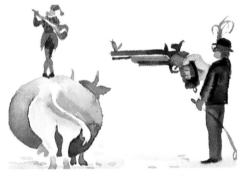

Real objects in real space relate to each other in scale.
Shapes representing them in a painting need to be in relative scale as well. For example, a tree can't be taller than the mountain it stands on; a rider can't be bigger than his horse; a handgun can't be as big as the man who holds it. Scale is played with in cartoons and caricatures.

Graphic Symbols

Graphic symbols are painted components intended to resemble something familiar to the conscious mind, but that may also have another meaning to the subconcious intellect. For example, the shape of a spruce tree not only looks like an evergreen, it also serves as a pointing arrow directing the viewer's attention away from itself. An orange oval is a colourful shape that may be read as the symbol of an autumn leaf.

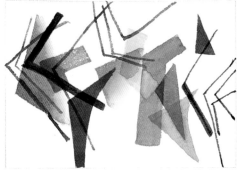

Directionals
Wedge shapes point like arrows.

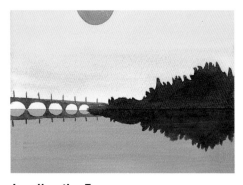

Leading the Eye
Curves, straight lines and repeating elements lead the eye as well.

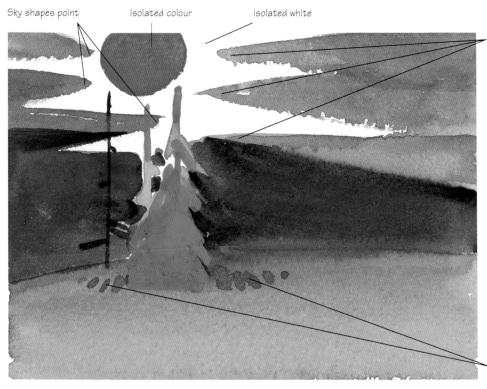

Sky shapes point

Isolated colour

Isolated white

Sky shapes point

Repetitive elements point

Too Many Pointers
If the viewer's attention lingers in one spot, maybe too many 'pointers' aim at that point. If that spot is on the edge of the painting, the viewer's eye may leave the composition.

Path of Vision

The human eye is incapable of reporting visual images to the brain fast enough to comprehend everything on a painting at one glance. The eyes have to roam through the surface from one area to another. This visual travel pattern is called the *path of vision*. It can be *instinctive* or *directed*. In a well composed painting the path of vision may be determined by skilfully arranged graphic symbols. The viewer's path of vision responds instinctively to the artist's directed signals.

The directed path of vision must be a subtle suggestion, not a roaring command. The viewer must be gently guided, not shoved through the painting by brute force.

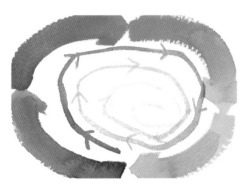

The Corkscrew Path

The ideal path of vision works as a corkscrew, moving in a circular motion toward infinity while touching all four sides and bypassing all four corners. The Western viewer's eye will usually move clockwise (left to right) because we read that way and our habit influences our behaviour.

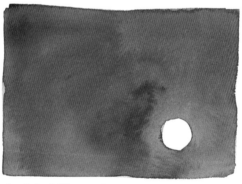

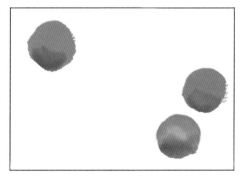

Isolated Elements

The viewer's first attention is directed to any isolated element, particularly to a bright colour or to a strongly contrasting spot. This attraction becomes even stronger if both conditions exist in the same location (above left). If several of these points are present in equal strength (above right), the eye will often select the lowest one first.

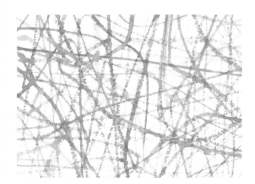

Overall Patterns

When the composition consists of pattern-like, equally important and evenly distributed elements, the path of vision usually begins at the bottom centre.

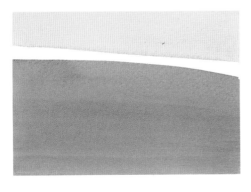

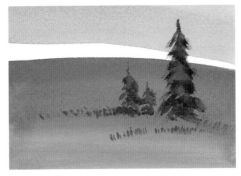

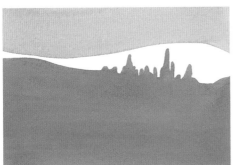

Edges

An undisturbed line across the painting is an obstacle to a comfortable path of vision (above left). An edge placed in this manner needs to be interrupted by graphic stoppers such as a crossing shape (above) or a varied edge (left).

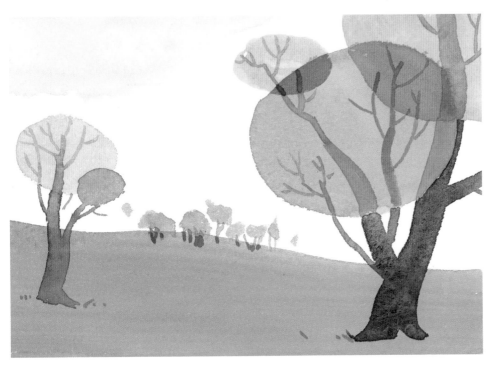

The visual journey, the corkscrew-like movement referred to earlier, is also a psychological journey for the viewer. Directing that journey is one way to communicate your feelings. But it is impossible to predict flawlessly the entire path of vision. It has to grow with the composition little by little as the painting progresses to its completion.

Path to the Distance

This visual journey extends not only up and down and sideways, but into the illusionary distance as well. In a realistic painting with depth, the artist must lead the viewer's eye in three dimensions.

Planes

White paper serves as a background for watercolour. It is flat and has only width and height, but after staring at it for a while, an illusion of depth will appear to the mind's eye. The artist can actually feel that the square space has planes – foreground, middle ground and background.

If a line is drawn across the paper, and the viewer concentrates on it for a while, the line will appear to be an edge where two planes meet. At first, both planes will look flat, but after a little more staring they will appear to be on a three-dimensional tilt bending away from or towards the viewer. The line between the two planes will appear to advance or recede.

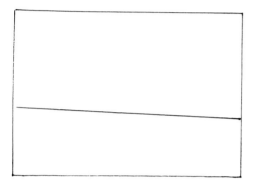

A Line, or Two Planes?
A line drawn across a white sheet of paper will take on the appearance of the division between two planes, perhaps sky and earth.

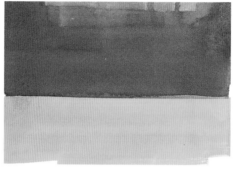

Add Complementary Colours
Flat washes of strongly contrasting (complementary) colours on the two planes will make the planes vibrate and create tension.

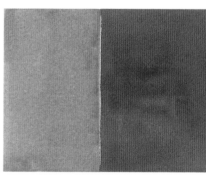

Add Analogous Colours
Two flat rectangles of similar tone occupied by analogous (related) colours feel quiet and agreeable.

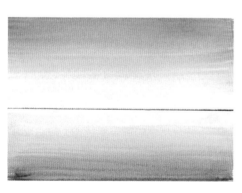

Shaded Planes
If planes are shaded until they seem to taper in each other's direction, subtle tension is created.

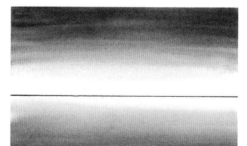

Balance
When they severely taper towards one another, they support (balance) each other.

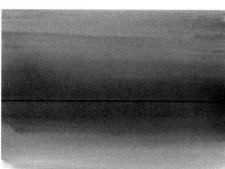

Active Imbalance
If they taper away from each other, an active imbalance occurs similar to a tug-of-war.

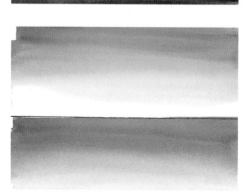

Parallel Planes
When both tilt in the same direction (parallel planes), both appear to be slipping away.

Wispy Clouds

For the graceful softness of these clouds, you need a dark background so the light shapes will show up. Your wash must be rich in consistency but not drippy. Timing is essential; measure it in seconds, not minutes.

In the techniques on pages 54–109, I use mostly Blockx colours with some Winsor & Newton exceptions that are identified as such.

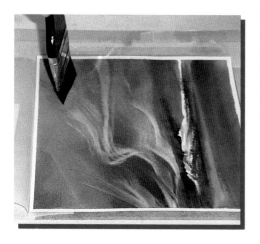

The 5cm (2in) wide, soft flat brush is held vertically, and the paper is just damp. Drag the brush through the moist colour with a back-and-forth twisting motion, while gradually and simultaneously releasing the pressure. Repeat this technique several times, wiping the brush clean after each application.

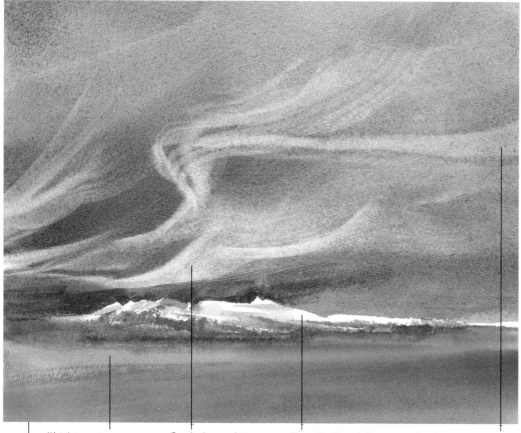

The sky is a loosely mixed wash of magenta, gold ochre, burnt sienna light, ultramarine blue deep and cyanine blue. I squeezed all the water I could out of a soft 5cm (2in) flat brush and rolled the edge of this thirsty brush with gentle pressure into the damp colour to lift out the wispy cloud shapes. After each contact I wiped the brush clean with a tissue, then repeated the action until I was satisfied. I did not touch the shape of the white mountains. I added the hint of grassy foreground with fast, decisive brush strokes using gold ochre and cyanine blue.

Wet-into-wet warm colour complement.

Brushed several times with a thirsty, damp brush.

Negative shape left white.

Brushed only once with a thirsty, damp brush.

The big difference between the sketch below and the sketch on the facing page is that the sky in this one is dominated by phthalo blue. The colour of the lifted clouds ended up blue because the phthalo blue is staining. In the first sketch, the sky is a neutral colour and therefore white after lifting out. In both cases, it is essential to wipe off the lifted colour and squeeze the brush dry after each contact with the damp paint. This way you won't dirty the lifted-out clouds.

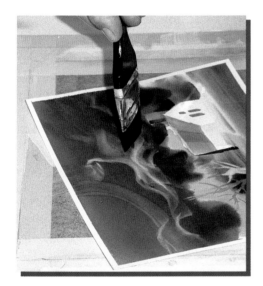

The paper is just moist, the shine just about to go dull when you move the 5cm (2in) wide, soft flat brush through the damp colour with a back-and-forth twisting motion, lifting off the light clouds. Press the damp and thirsty brush a little harder at first, then release the pressure gradually until the brush is completely off the surface. Repeat this several times, wiping the brush clean each time.

Thirsty, damp brush marks rolled into damp colour.

Simultaneously applied dark cool and light warm colours.

Overlapping thirsty, damp brush marks.

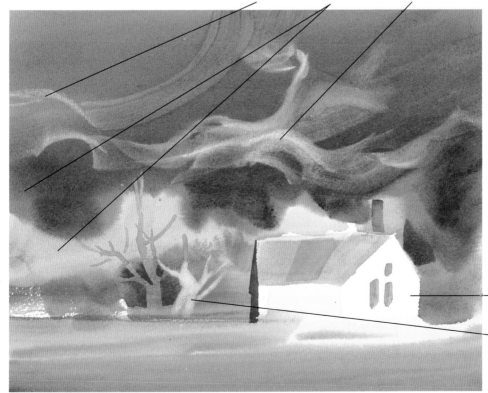

The dark sky is a combination of phthalo blue and a touch of gold ochre. I swept out the clouds in the same way as in the first picture. The very dark sky creates strong contrast and intense drama. The shape of the house was left white, and the trees behind it as well as the foreground were washed with gold ochre, rose madder and phthalo blue in varied combinations.

Negative shape left paper-white.

Light shape lifted out after drying. Phthalo blue staining dominance.

Cumulus Clouds

Because the soft edges of the white clouds are painted with a strong staining colour, the edges must be achieved with dark colours and decisively made marks. Don't expect to go back and fix them; you won't get away with it because of the staining nature of the pigment. If you lift the colour later you'll get a blue tint.

Area left pure white.

Simultaneously painted warm colours.

Phthalo blue-dominated dark wash on wet paper.

Burnt sienna and ultramarine blue combination.

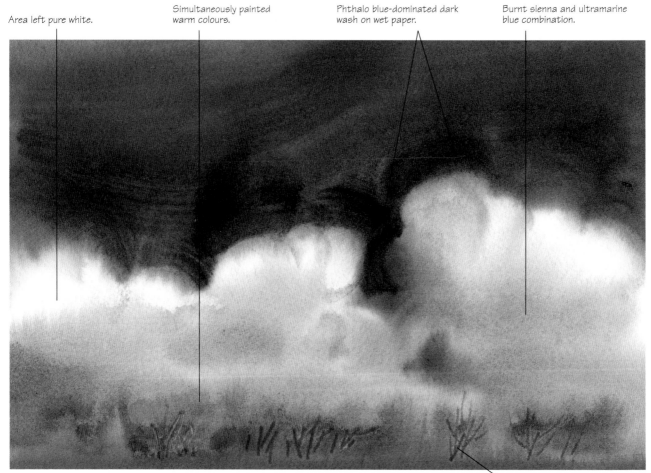

Lines scraped into wet paint with the point of a round brush handle.

On a wet paper using a 2.5cm (1in) slant bristle brush loaded with a very rich mix of phthalo blue and Winsor & Newton sepia, I painted round the top edges of the white clouds. Because my paint was very thick, the edges simply softened, but stayed readable on the damp paper. For the bottom section of the clouds, I painted the grey mixed from burnt sienna and ultramarine blue. I dropped in a bit of green grassy area (phthalo blue and gamboge yellow) and hinted at a few autumn trees (gamboge yellow and burnt sienna). The darker lines indicating tree trunks at the bottom were scraped into the still-wet paint with the round point of a small brush handle.

Stratus Clouds

The light colours must be built up by going from the white of the paper to light colours, and to darker colours last. Each time you darken the tone, think of the light shape next to the brush stroke. Think of the negative shapes while you paint the positive strokes.

Several medium-dark glazes.

Light-glazed repetitive shapes.

Dark colours applied last.

White paper left untouched.

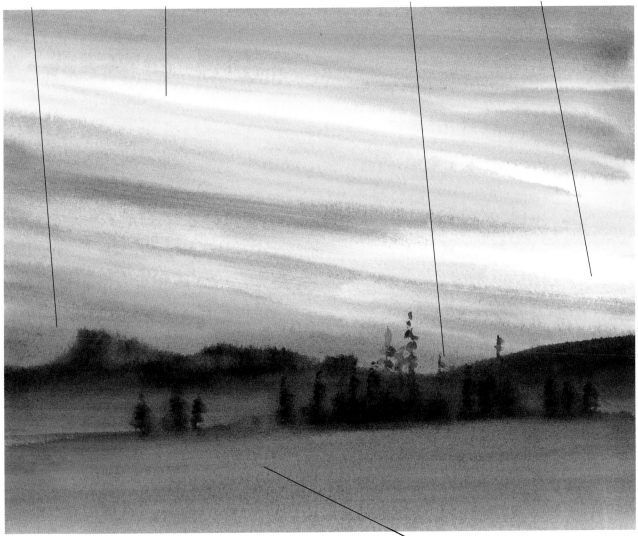

Warmer ground colour.

On a wet surface, I treated the windswept clouds as negative shapes. Negative shapes are 'left out'. They are defined by painting darker colours next to or round them. I brushed in a combination of three analogous colours: ultramarine and cyanine blues and phthalo green in varied dominance. For the dark edge of the middle ground, I applied phthalo green, ultramarine blue and rose madder, plus a little gamboge yellow for the grassy foreground.

Dramatic Clouds

This effect requires a colour removal technique. Don't leave your wet colours on the paper too long before you use the tissue to lift them off. The more quickly you act, the whiter the clouds will look. It is important to change the tissue after each contact with the paper to prevent reprinting the colour you have just lifted off.

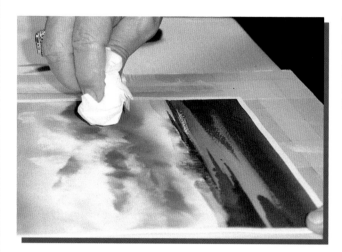

The wash is shiny wet, but not dripping. Repeatedly press the bunched-up paper tissue into the wet paint, lifting off the cloud shapes. Repeat the contact but turn the tissue each time to make sure that only its fresh and clean part touches the paint.

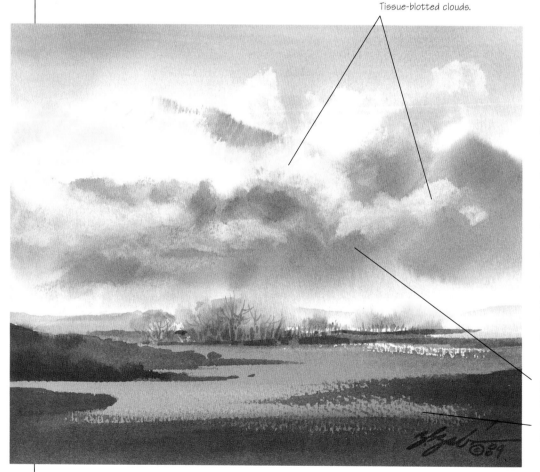

Tissue-blotted clouds.

Original dark blue wash on wet paper.

Drybrush stroke.

My colours were cyanine blue, rose madder, burnt sienna and gamboge yellow. I painted the sky and the high mountains on a wet surface simultaneously. Cyanine blue, rose madder and a touch of burnt sienna supplied the right combination for the background. I lifted out the white clouds by pressing a bunched-up paper tissue into the wet paint. The tissue absorbs the water and paint immediately and surface-dries the paper wherever it touches it. I also dropped in the warm-coloured autumn trees and several glazes of dark warm washes in the foreground to show colour perspective.

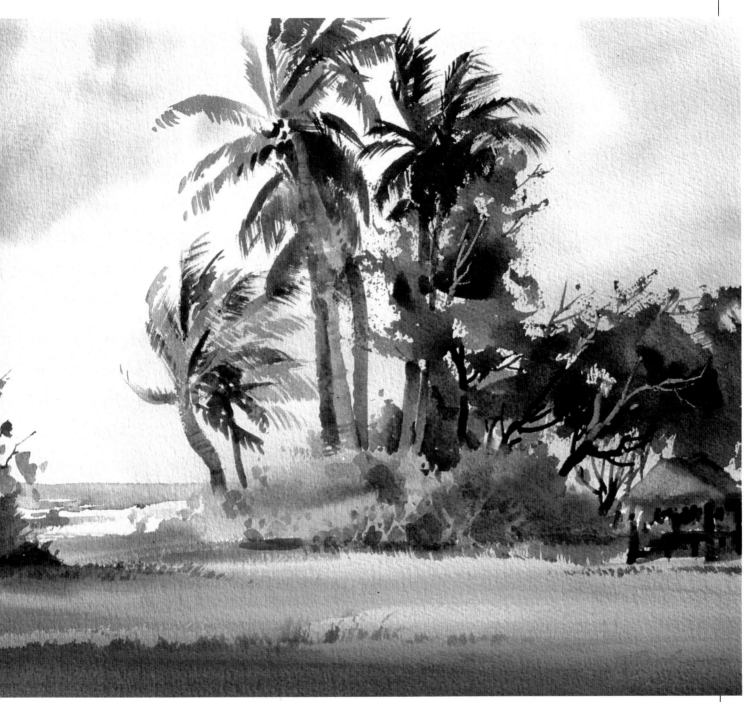

One of the most important sections of this Hawaiian painting is the sky. To indicate breezes, I established the windblown clouds by *not* painting them. I painted the blue sky round them on wet paper, leaving the clouds' edges soft. Against this light background I painted the contrasting palm trees, their branches bending with the wind. These branches were painted with a slant bristle brush loaded with rich pigment and little water. I drybrushed most of the dark vegetation in cool shadow colours. Lastly, I painted the sunny foreground with warm dominance on the grass. The exciting pattern of the tropical trees shows up well against the simple but fresh background.

Trade Wind
38x56cm (15x22in)

Birch Trees

This technique can be used to paint many kinds of light bark, especially against a dark background. The colour you choose for your background will affect the colour of the light trees. Because rose madder (a light staining colour) dominated the area where I removed the shapes of the light birches in the background, its staining dominance shows up even after the colour is squeezed off. Whatever light colour you want to show in the scraped-out shape, that's the one that must dominate the background colour to start with.

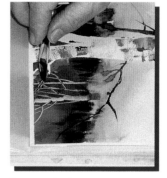

On a wet background, press the slanted edge of the tip of a plastic brush handle as hard as you can, squeezing off the light shapes of the young birches and their branches. Hold the brush handle with your thumb and forefinger but deliver the pressure with your wrist.

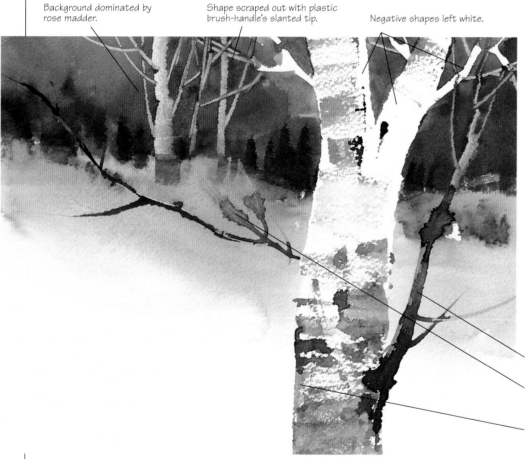

Background dominated by rose madder.

Shape scraped out with plastic brush-handle's slanted tip.

Negative shapes left white.

Painted with palette knife.

Palette knife line contacting damp area.

Palette knife-smeared dry-brush texture.

I started with a rich, dark background painted onto dry paper, leaving a negative shape for the large foreground tree. My colours were gold ochre, rose madder and ultramarine blue deep. While this thick wash was still tacky wet, I lifted off the distant birch trunks with the tip of my plastic brush handle. Then I was ready to 'drybrush' the texture of the birch bark by quickly dragging across the colours with the edge of my palette knife. I applied the larger branches with the tip of my vertically held palette knife, allowing the liquid paint to flow off as I moved the knife away from the trunk.

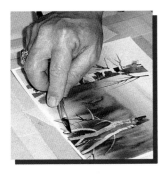

While the background wash is still wet, use the slanted tip of the brush handle to remove the birch-tree shape. Hold the brush with a firm grip and press with your wrist as hard as you can. Hold the flat, oval part of the brush handle at a 45° angle to squeeze the colour off smoothly without ripping the wet paper.

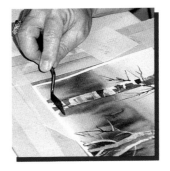

Tap the palette knife's edge and its flat back onto the dry white paper in order to do the peel marks and the drybrush texture at the same time. Use varied liquid colours. Wet paint produces solid shapes; the less water in the paint, the finer the texture.

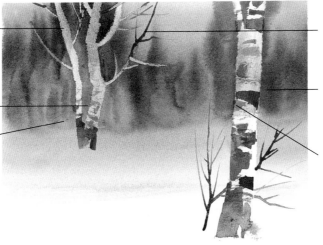

Staining blue showing through scraped-out light shape.

Warm tone was added after background colour had dried.

Wet, warm colours flooded into wet, cool colours.

'Positive' branch shape was painted last with rigger.

Background was painted first, leaving tree trunks white.

Colourful drybrush shapes were added last.

Though the procedure here was similar to the sketch on the left, this time the background was painted with a *varied* dominance. As you can see, the scraped-out light birch retained the same characteristics in much lighter tones. The longer you wait to do the scraping, the more time the settling colours have to stain the paper, reducing the contrast somewhat.

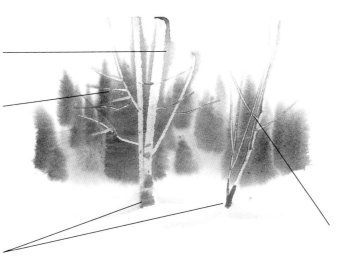

Overflow of colour moved from lower, dark background colours by brush handle.

Branches scraped out with back of brush handle.

Warm accents against cool dominance.

Here I left the upper third of the painting white. As I squeezed the colour off, the brush handle acted like a small bulldozer pushing the wet colour in front of itself. In a dark background this colour simply blends away. However, here the colour was deposited on the wet, white background as the brush handle entered it. This free and loose accent engaged the edge and prevented the sketch from becoming an unpleasant vignette design.

Branch shapes were scraped out with brush handle while paper was damp, but not wet.

Pine Branches

Most pine branches have little elbows close to the trunk, and the needles grow upwards from the branches which hold them up with their finger-tips, as it were. The top of the needle clusters need to be painted with a richly loaded dry brush flipped upwards and away from the paper to show the needle-like finish. Complete these brush strokes quickly and decisively. Don't pick at them.

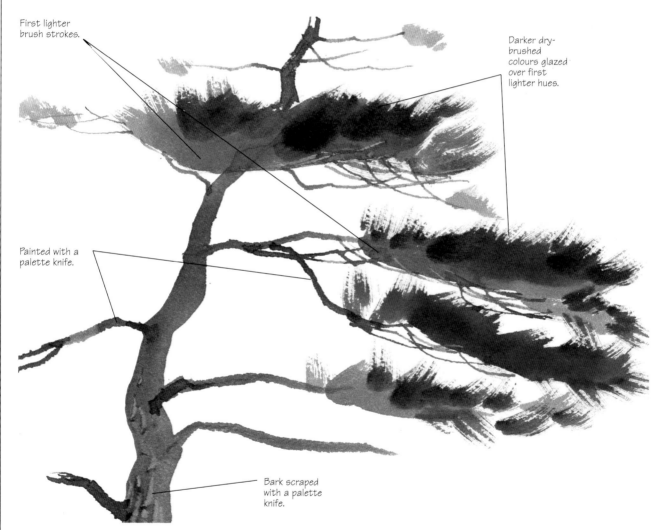

First lighter brush strokes.

Darker dry-brushed colours glazed over first lighter hues.

Painted with a palette knife.

Bark scraped with a palette knife.

I painted the branches with my palette knife using liquid-consistency paint. The foliage was drybrushed with a 5cm (2in) bristle brush filled with dark paint. My colours were gold ochre, magenta, phthalo green and ultramarine blue deep.

Lifted-out White Trees

The clarity of the white trees is the direct result of my choice of an efficient tool: my nail clipper. The tip of its handle is very firm, but smooth, so it will not tear the wet paper. Avoid ripping the surface by choosing a smooth tool that lets you press very hard. Any thin, light lines against a dark background can be done with this technique. Frosty weeds, birch, aspen or sycamore branches, or white whiskers on an old man are just a few examples. Think of techniques as principles, not isolated subjects.

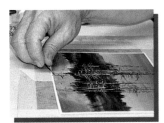

This group of bleached-out light trees is formed by scraping them out of a very dark and still-damp background with the handle of a nail clipper. Hold it between your thumb and fingers and press as hard as you can with the strength coming from the wrist. Scrape the thin shapes with rapidly moving strokes before the background has a chance to dry too much.

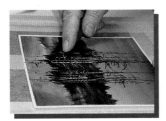

The same effect may be achieved by holding a small pocket-knife blade point on its side, guided by the index finger, while removing the light shapes with heavy pressure.

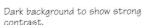

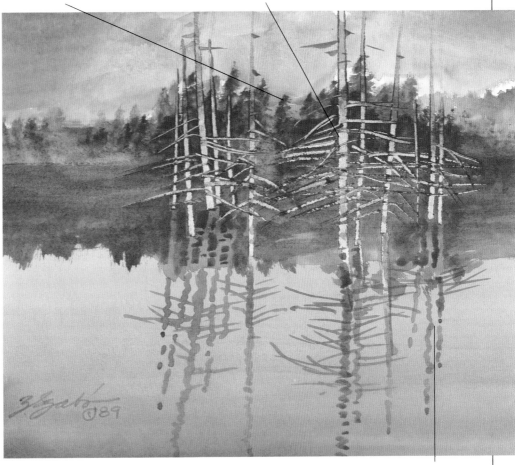

Dark background to show strong contrast.

Scraped out with the smooth tip of a nail-clipper handle.

Glazed reflections.

This little landscape started with the basic washes for the sky and water. My colours were cyanine blue, gold ochre and rose madder. With the same colours in a rich creamy consistency, I quickly washed in the warm-dominated trees on the distant shore and their reflection using my 5cm (2in) bristle brush. While this shape was still quite wet, I pressed the tip of my nail-clipper handle very hard to remove the shapes of the light trees and their branches. I finished on the dry surface by painting the wiggly reflections with my rigger brush.

Weeds

To paint this colourful clump of weeds, I first washed in the neutral background colour. The initial silhouette of the weed clump was painted on the dry white paper and into the still-damp wash at the top simultaneously. The edges stayed sharp on the dry surfaces but blurred when they touched the moist colour. If your dark colour is rich enough and you apply the colour very fast, the difference will be negligible. The scraped-out weeds look colourful because the dark colour behind them is dominated with separate charged colours. Therefore, the light weeds show whatever dominant colours are underneath them.

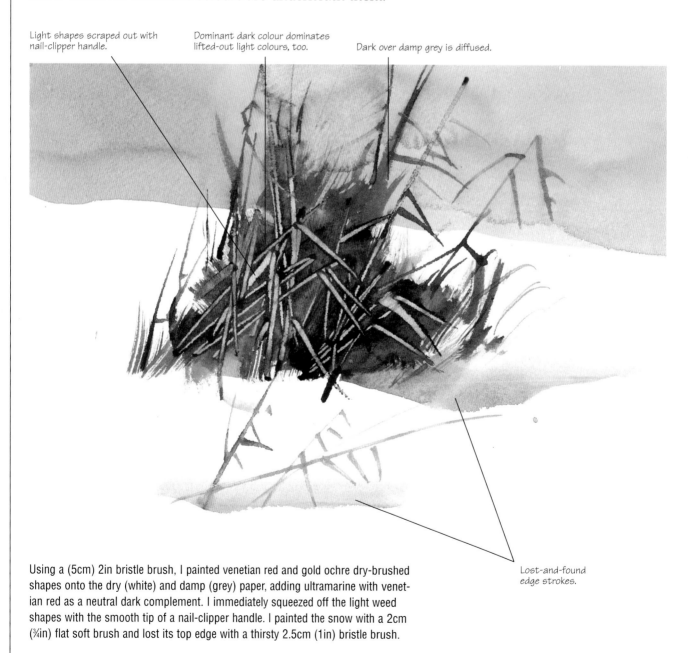

Light shapes scraped out with nail-clipper handle.

Dominant dark colour dominates lifted-out light colours, too.

Dark over damp grey is diffused.

Lost-and-found edge strokes.

Using a (5cm) 2in bristle brush, I painted venetian red and gold ochre dry-brushed shapes onto the dry (white) and damp (grey) paper, adding ultramarine with venetian red as a neutral dark complement. I immediately squeezed off the light weed shapes with the smooth tip of a nail-clipper handle. I painted the snow with a 2cm (¾in) flat soft brush and lost its top edge with a thirsty 2.5cm (1in) bristle brush.

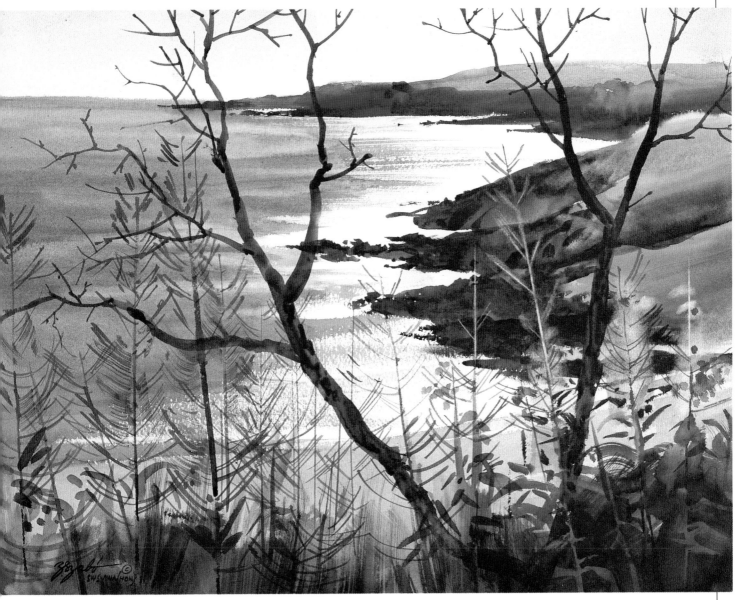

The calm but rugged coastline provides a high-contrast background to the delicate fireweeds and their accompanying dark branches. I painted the sky, the coastal hills, and their rocky shores first. Then I glazed the mid-tone sea with a glazing technique on dry paper. I moved my brush horizontally and lifted it gradually as I approached the coastal rocks. The resulting drybrush leads the eye to the white shimmer. Over the lighter parts of the background near the bottom edge, I painted the colourful lace of the fireweeds. Where they crossed a dark area, I lifted out the background with a wet scrub-and-blot technique. I glazed the weeds' leaves with dark glazes and finished the painting with the dark tree and its fine branches.

Scottish Autumn
34.25x44.5cm (13½x17½in)

Flowering Trees

Here is a quick wet-into-wet technique. The dark background is painted first on wet paper, leaving the soft main shape (in this case, the flowering tree) as a negative shape. For this or any similar subject, make sure that the negative shape stays perfectly white while you paint the dark colour around it. Use less water in your brush than there is on the paper. To get the soft mauve colour, the flowering tree had to be painted on white, not dirty, paper.

Wet-into-wet shapes with independent colour dominance.

Negative shape surrounded by darker, wet shapes.

Lines painted with rigger brush.

While the paper was wet, I painted round the flowering tree shape. The sky colour came from cyanine blue and phthalo green. For the grey on the left, I added a little rose madder and gamboge yellow. I painted the dark evergreens phthalo green, gamboge yellow, and rose madder. As the surface was losing its shine, I dropped little rosettes of water and a small amount of rose madder into the irregular white shape left for the flowering foliage, using a No. 5 rigger brush. The trunks and branches were added when the paper was almost dry. Note that I surrounded the flowers with the darkest colours to exaggerate the contrast.

When these few hints are applied, they can cause an exciting interaction between the suggested planes. Representational details should enhance, not distract, from this relationship.

Balance is the key to good composition. Any elements with overpowering visual attraction will disturb unless they are balanced with complements. Well balanced elements will induce an exciting play of tension in the painting. Lack of balance creates tension, causing the viewer to leave the composition.

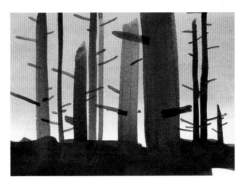

Narrow Vertical Planes
Narrow vertical planes close together resist each other, creating independent strength for each.

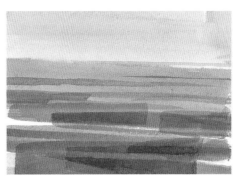

Narrow Horizontal Planes
If the same narrow planes are placed horizontally, they feel comfortably stable and calming.

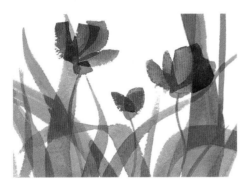

Illusion of Movement
Overlapping transparent shapes create the illusion of movement.

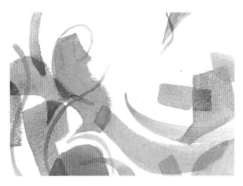

Similar Tones
The eye travels more easily from one shape to another when the shapes are close in tone and colour.

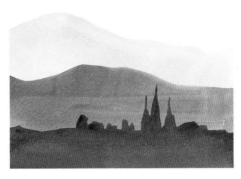

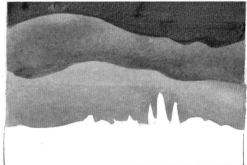

Planes have different tones and colour temperatures
These qualities define their distance and clarify their location in space. Generally, dark tones and warm colours make a plane appear near, while light tones and cool colours make it recede. This rule may reverse when planes overlap.

These two diagrams show the same basic shapes, but with the colours of the planes reversed. Notice how discomforting the illustration on the right is. Because warm dark tones generally appear near, the position of the brownish plane is very hard to fit into our habitual ways of thinking.

CHAPTER 4

Basic Techniques at a Glance

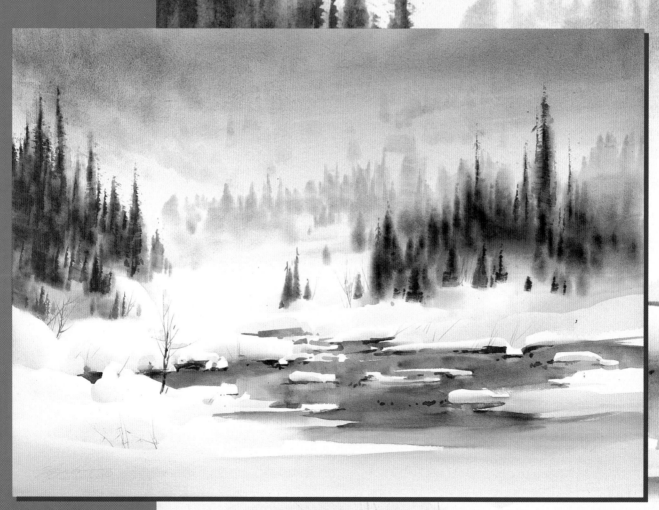

Snow Cocktail
48x71cm (19x28in)
Collection of Papierfabriek
Shut Bv.

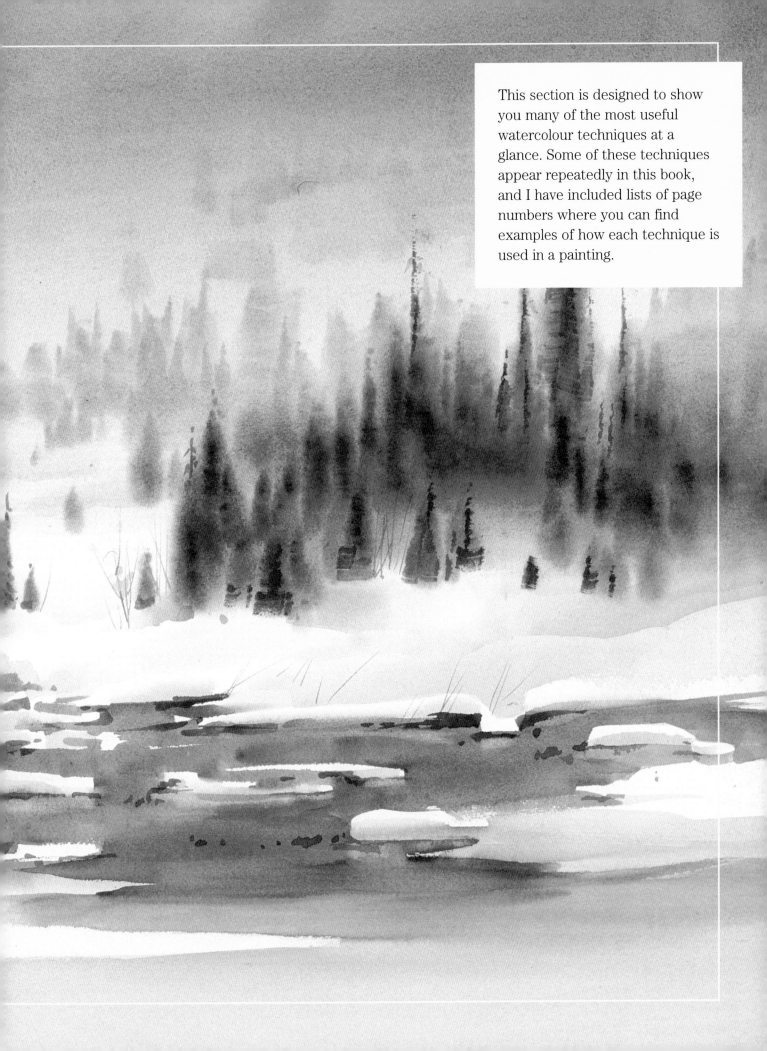

This section is designed to show you many of the most useful watercolour techniques at a glance. Some of these techniques appear repeatedly in this book, and I have included lists of page numbers where you can find examples of how each technique is used in a painting.

Flooding a Wash

A *wash* is the application of wet water-colour to a shape or area. The paper may be dry or pre-moistened, but the applied wet colour is still called a wash.

Flooding a wet wash means that another colour is painted into a wet wash with plenty of paint as well as water in the brush. If the flooded colour is lighter than the original wash, the application may have to be repeated several times before the new colour can truly replace the first one. In this case the brush needs to be rinsed and wiped clean after each contact with the first wash to prevent polluting the new colour.

To make sure that the brush is capable of holding lots of water, use a soft, full-haired brush.

Lost-and-Found Edges

When a wet brush stroke is painted onto a dry paper surface, all its edges are sharp. Each edge reads equally well. Shortly after application of the stroke, a thirsty, damp brush can be dragged through one edge to blend it away. This brush needs to be dry enough to soak up some of the wet colour on contact, but wide enough and wet enough to moisten the dry paper next to the stroke.

I find a slant bristle brush ideally suited for this job. Its hairs cling together and tend not to hold much water, but when pressed a little, it will dampen the dry paper in its path as well as absorb some of the wet colour. However, any brush can do the job with just a little practice. Make sure that the thirsty brush is dampened with crystal-clear water to lose the edge completely.

The descriptive name comes from the fact that as you blend one edge it will 'lose' its importance and will simultaneously 'find' the other sharp edge as a strongly visible element.

More examples of flooding a wash are shown on pages:

68 Jagged Granite Rocks

88 Background Forest

98 Flooded Washes

99 Colourful Darks

104 Rock Setting

107 Soft Lifted-out Trees

More examples of lost-and-found edges are shown on pages:

70 Rolling Surf

77 Trees in Heavy Snow

78 Young Spruce in Snow

82 Mist

90 Winter Island

96 Negative Shapes

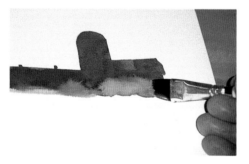

A light colour is flooded into a dark wash.

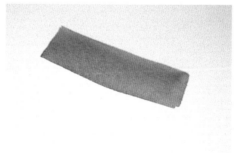

A stroke is laid down with a flat brush.

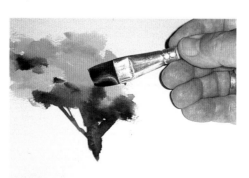

A dark colour is flooded into a light wash.

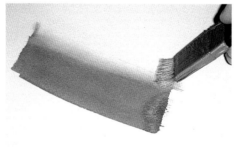

A thirsty, damp slant (or straight-cut) bristle brush dampens the dry paper and absorbs some of the colour, softening one edge.

Wet-and-Blot Lifting

When a large area is painted with a dark colour, small areas can be removed to reveal light shapes with this technique. If the colour is a nonstaining combination, a soft or bristle brush can be used. However, if the colour is somewhat staining or strongly staining, a firm bristle brush is necessary to get the job done.

In both cases the brush must be *dripping* with clean water. With the wet brush, scrub the desired area until the friction and the water loosen the dry pigment. Immediately absorb the liquid with a bunched-up tissue, removing the loose pigment with the water. Under no circumstances should you allow the loose colour to sit on the scrubbed surface for any length of time. It might soak back into the fibres of the paper, never to lift again.

Not having enough water in the scrubbing brush invites disaster. A merely damp brush can only rough up the surface and will actually scrub the paint *into* the paper. Part of a large scrubbed shape may start drying before you have a chance to blot it, so it's better to scrub small areas at a time. It won't take long to loosen and remove the colour on these small sections, and by repeating this step, you can spread the small shapes slowly until all the desired area is lifted.

Back Runs

I am sure you've heard the term, *happy accidents*. A back run is one of the most common and exciting of these. It happens when an already-applied colour is drying and some extra water touches the wash.

When water comes in contact with a colour that is almost surface dry but the paper underneath is still damp, the underlying paper attracts the water and causes it to spread rapidly. As the water expands, it moistens the applied paint from the bottom, causing it to move with the water. As soon as the volume of water cannot spread any further, it stops, and the colour is deposited on the perimeter of the shape as a darker outline.

When this happens accidentally you have several choices: incorporate it into the design, try to repair it or start again. My first choice is to try to use it as a new design element, second is to repair it after it dries, last is to abandon ship.

I think of the back run as an expansion of wet technique and use it to excite my painting. Because the timing must be exactly right, you have about thirty to sixty seconds in which to act. Don't try to be perfect during this short period, just go for it. The more water you use, the wider the back run will spread. Practise this with a daring attitude. The darker the background, the more the back-run shape will contrast with it.

More examples of wet-and-blot lifting are shown on pages:

72 Shadows on Snow
73 Shadows on Snow
75 Warmly Lit Snow
80 Heavy Fog

More examples of back runs are shown on pages:

77 Trees in Heavy Snow
88 Background Forest
90 Winter Island
93 Frost on Trees
98 Flooded Washes
103 Tree Impressions

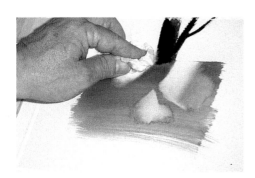

A wet brush scrubs the nonstaining colour, which is immediately blotted up with a clean tissue.

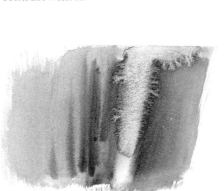

You can see the colour sediments deposited all around the edge of the wet area. The result is a back run.

Brush-handle Scraping

The tip end of some soft-haired, flat brush handles are cut on a slant to accommodate scraping. This slanted edge is very useful when you need to scrape a sharp, light shape out of a moist, and usually dark, background.

Because of the oval shape of the slanted end, the longer edge can scrape out a wider shape while the tip will remove a narrow line. For example, the broad side can scrape out a tree trunk and the tip will look after the branches.

When using this handy little tool, press hard but not so hard that you break the edge. Remember, it is only a plastic material; don't treat it like metal. However, if you should accidentally chip it, you can recover a new edge if you sandpaper it.

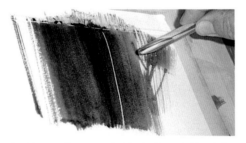

A wide area is scraped with the broad side of the handle.

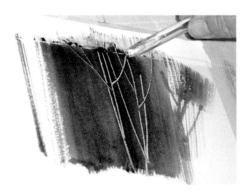

Narrow lines are scraped with the tip of the handle.

Using a Palette Knife

The function of this little tool is twofold: It can *apply* or *remove* colour. First, be sure you have a palette knife like the one shown. It is important that the handle stem has a bend in it to accommodate your fingers as they grip the handle. Because the metal blade is treated with greasy material to protect it during storage, you need to clean it with toothpaste before use. The blade must allow water (liquid paint) to adhere to its surface.

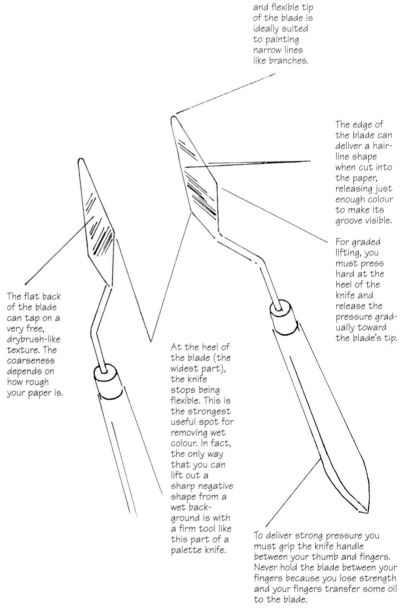

The rounded and flexible tip of the blade is ideally suited to painting narrow lines like branches.

The edge of the blade can deliver a hairline shape when cut into the paper, releasing just enough colour to make its groove visible.

For graded lifting, you must press hard at the heel of the knife and release the pressure gradually toward the blade's tip.

The flat back of the blade can tap on a very free, drybrush-like texture. The coarseness depends on how rough your paper is.

At the heel of the blade (the widest part), the knife stops being flexible. This is the strongest useful spot for removing wet colour. In fact, the only way that you can lift out a sharp negative shape from a wet background is with a firm tool like this part of a palette knife.

To deliver strong pressure you must grip the knife handle between your thumb and fingers. Never hold the blade between your fingers because you lose strength and your fingers transfer some oil to the blade.

Lifting Out Colour

This technique can be used under two different conditions: lifting colour from a *moist* surface or from a *dry* surface.

Before a freshly applied wash dries, while it is still damp, the colour is vulnerable to touch. If a thirsty (damp) brush, paper tissue or anything solid touches the wash, it will leave a mark. Repeated brushing at this stage with a brush dipped in clean water may recover the paper close to white, unless the colours are staining.

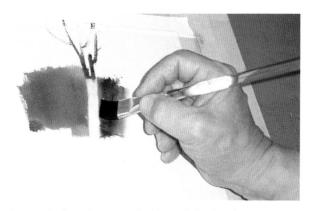

The tree trunk shape is removed with a soft flat brush.

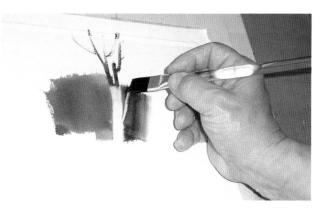

A smaller branch is removed by stroking upwards with the flat tip of the brush.

Luminous Opaque Colours

Even though watercolour purists will deny using opaque colours, they will quietly admit to painting with cadmiums, ochre, cerulean and a few other colours that fall into the category of opaque pigments. Opaque colours, except the very dark ones, are reflective. This means they are capable of reflecting light from their surface, while the transparent hues let the light go through to the paper and the paper supplies the reflected light that makes them glow. Some of the most intense colours are opaque by definition, but we still use them diluted with water. This way they are almost transparent, but when they are glazed over other colours, they may partly cover them.

With some subjects, such as fog, the opacity of a colour imitates the behaviour of Nature. Fog is a filter, like a semi-opaque wash. Fog makes white objects behind it look darker; so can an opaque colour. Fog covers dark objects to some extent; opaque paint does, too.

Some colours are reflective enough to do the job by themselves: cobalt blue, cerulean blue, naples yellow, for example.

Titanium white is a very useful ingredient for a semi-opaque wash. It mixes with any of the colours and transfers its softening qualities even to the most transparent hue. It does a good job as a glaze on top of a dry colour, or it can be mixed with other colours.

More examples of using a brush handle are shown on pages:

61 Birch Trees
81 Heavy Fog
99 Colourful Darks
104 Rock Setting

More examples of lifted-out colour are shown on pages:

54 Wispy Clouds
55 Wispy Clouds
85 Cobweb
107 Soft Lifted-out Trees

More examples of using a palette knife are shown on pages:

61 Birch Trees
62 Pine Branches
68 Jagged Granite Rocks
69 Rounded Glacial Rocks
77 Trees in Heavy Snow
91 Rolling Snowbanks
100 Smooth Tree Bark
101 Rough Tree Bark
102 Glazed Tree Bark
104 Rock Setting
105 Palette Knife Trees

More examples of the luminous use of opaque colours are shown on pages:

80 Heavy Fog
81 Heavy Fog
83 Mist

CHAPTER 5

Watercolour Techniques for Painting

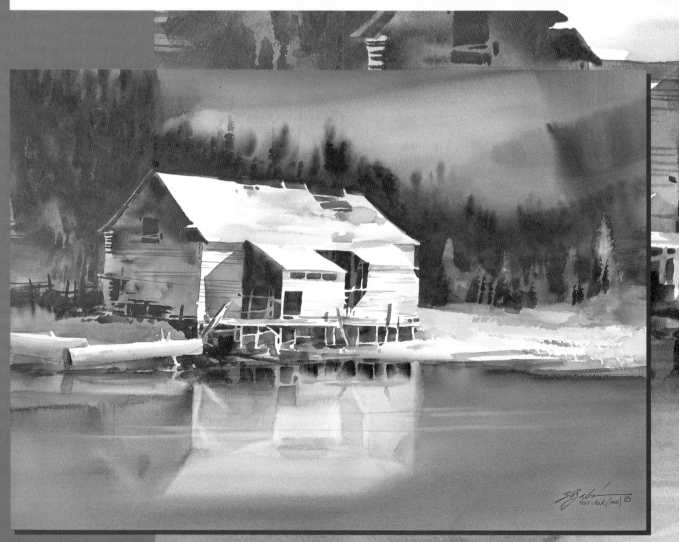

Pacific Castle
48x71cm (19x28in)
Collection of Eric
and Nancy Slagle.

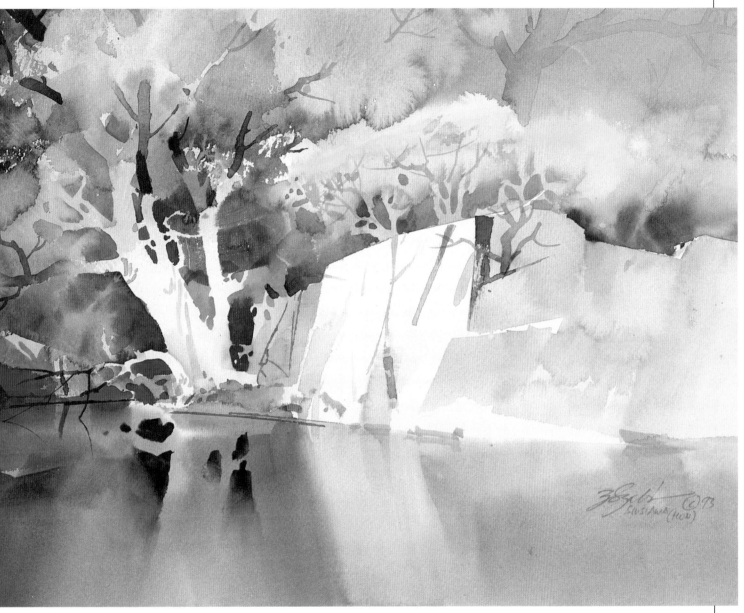

In this painting the dominant strength of white surrounded with rich, dark tones and colourful shapes created a powerful focal point. Starting on dry paper, I carefully painted round the white network of rocks and the big white tree. I painted the foliage and the background with several colourful glazes, allowing some of them to create loose back runs suggesting foliage clusters. My darks evolved gradually next to the whites to emphasize their brilliance. After all the images were finished, I painted the water and the reflections in a medium tone, with a few dark accents where my contrasting focal point needed it.

Happy Glow
38x51cm (15x 20in)
Collection of David
and Bonnie Hauck.

Jagged Granite Rocks

Here's another chance to use your palette knife to describe shapes. But remember: you must hold the knife firmly by its handle while your wrist delivers the necessary heavy pressure. Never hold the blade with your fingers; they aren't strong enough to squeeze off the colours. Use the widest and firmest part of the blade (the heel) because that is where the metal is firm enough to do the job.

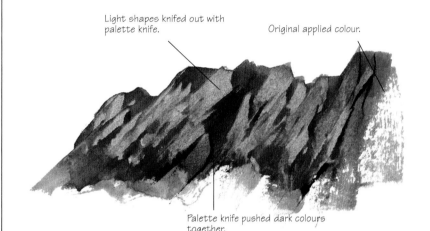

Light shapes knifed out with palette knife.

Original applied colour.

Palette knife pushed dark colours together.

The shapes of these rocks were painted as a silhouette with rich colours. I used a 2cm (¾in) soft flat brush for the colour application. The edge of the palette knife was pressed hard and moved downwards, squeezing off the light, flat shapes and depositing dark colour that looks like shaded crevices. Whatever colour dominated the initial wash will dominate the squeezed-off area as well.

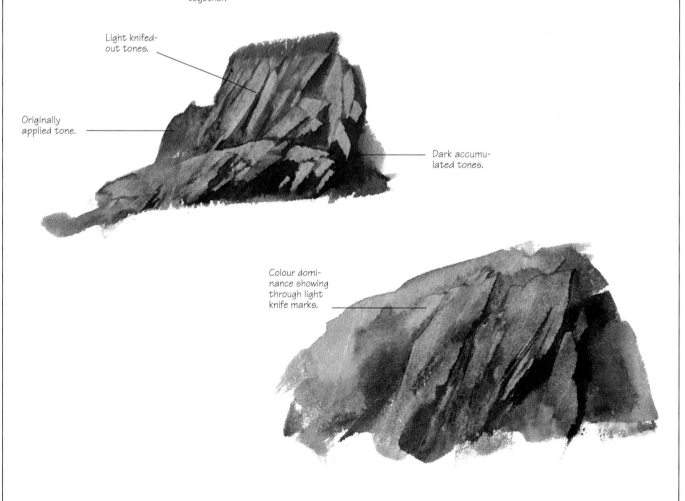

Light knifed-out tones.

Originally applied tone.

Dark accumulated tones.

Colour dominance showing through light knife marks.

Rounded Glacial Rocks

These rounded rock shapes are similar to the jagged rocks, but the movement of the palette knife is different. For the best results use paint with a thick, creamy consistency for these shapes. Holding the knife by the heel and with the tip pointing down, press hard at the heel and lift gently towards the tip while lifting off the colour. This tilt will produce the textured transition from the lightest to the darkest tone. If your colour is too runny, the wet pigment may gush back into the path of the knife.

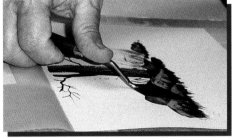

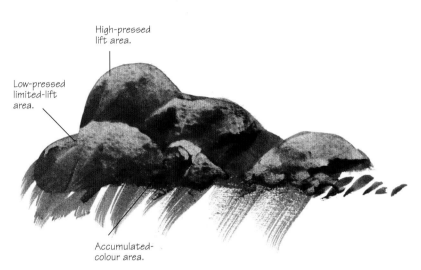

High-pressed lift area.

Low-pressed limited-lift area.

Accumulated-colour area.

The dark background wash should be a tacky consistency. Then knife off the light tones on the rocks with the wide, firm, pointed heel of a palette knife. Grip the handle of the knife with your fingers and apply the pressure with your thumb. Don't use your fingers on the blade for pressure. The thumb must carry the pressure from the wrist to the handle for best results.

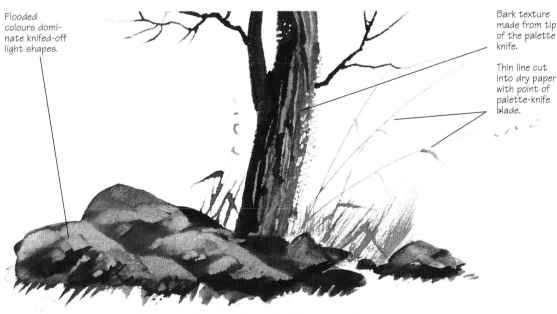

Flooded colours dominate knifed-off light shapes.

Bark texture made from tip of the palette knife.

Thin line cut into dry paper with point of palette-knife blade.

These rounded rocks were all painted with a 2cm (¾in) soft, flat brush and textured with the heel of the palette knife. I used complementary colours to establish their natural colour shape and tone. My colours were ultramarine blue, rose madder, gold ochre, burnt sienna and Winsor & Newton sepia. I did not *scrape* wet colour off, but *squeezed* it off with the firm heel of my brush.

Rolling Surf

It is hard to work out exactly what rolling waves look like because they constantly move. As the wave rolls over, its top edge is sharper and straighter and the bottom edge is broken up and more curved. This 'lace' effect is best painted with the flat side of a soft brush used as a dry-brush. While doing this, press very lightly. The bottom edge is a free shape. Let the brush show off the looseness of its natural hit-and-miss tendency.

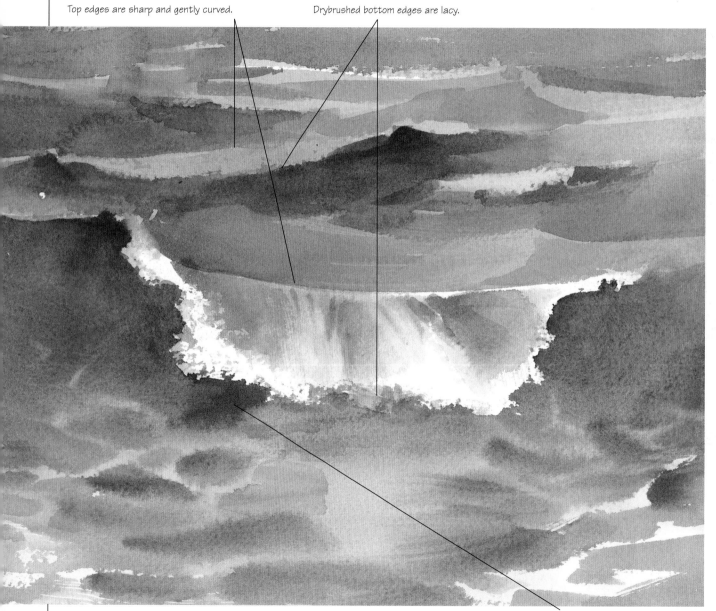

Top edges are sharp and gently curved.

Drybrushed bottom edges are lacy.

Darkest colour next to foamy white.

I painted the surf as if it were a tube-like wave. I brushed on rich glazes quickly and allowed some of the surf to stay white. I added a quick touch of dark to the damp, lacy underside and another one to the top edge of the white shape. My colours were cyanine blue, gold ochre, emerald green and Vandyke brown.

Puddle Reflections

The shapes of puddles are viewed in a foreshortened perspective. Many students, knowing that puddles are often round, fail to flatten them enough, as they would look when viewed from a normal viewpoint. These flat shapes may be pointed or oval, but are never a circle. Puddles make the best design elements when they contrast strongly with what is around them. If they are the same tone as the surface next to them, they don't stand out and you are better off leaving them out.

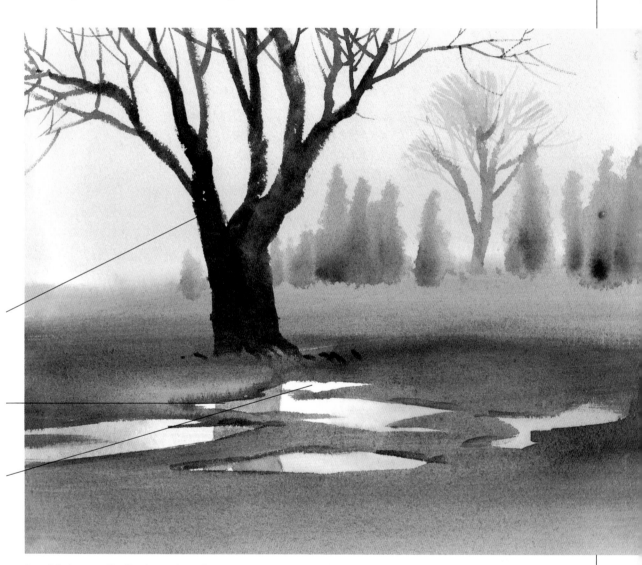

Dominant dark tone.

Reflection dominated by darkest tone and colour of the local colour (mud).

Negative shapes were left clear.

A puddle is a small reflective surface. The colour and tone of the *reflection* of the tree combines with the local colour, in this case the light grey muddy bottom of the puddle, which is lighter than the tree trunk or even the soil. Therefore the reflection of the tree is lighter than the tree itself. My colours were ultramarine blue, rose madder, phthalo green, and gold ochre. Note how the reflecting surface stops abruptly at the edge of the puddle.

Shadows on Snow

This technique is very sensitive to the brand of paper you use and the brand and choice of colour. It works best on a well sized surface with artists' quality nonstaining watercolour. Check the definition of nonstaining colours on page 21.

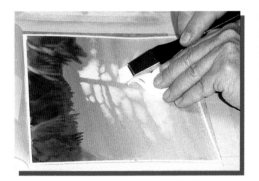

On the dry shadow colour use a small bristle brush loaded with clean water to remove the colour and show patches of sunlight. To make the blurry edges, move the brush faster and for a shorter time, blotting off the floating pigments immediately.

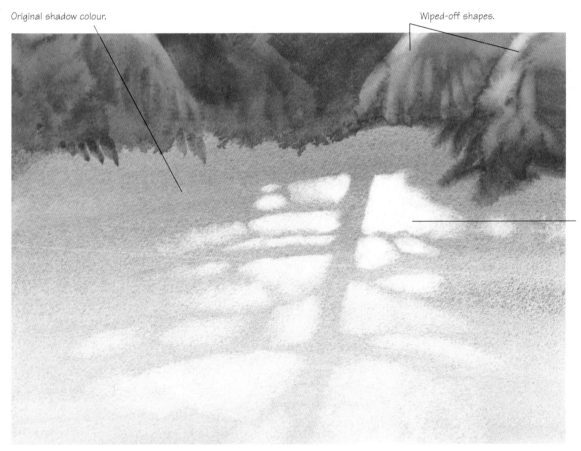

Original shadow colour.

Wiped-off shapes.

Islands of light shapes lifted out of a wash of nonstaining colours.

I painted the snow surface as if all of it were in shade, using manganese blue with a touch of cobalt violet on the dry paper surface. After the colour had dried completely, I treated the shadows as negative shapes and removed the sunlight shapes by loosening the dry paint with a very wet, small oil-painting brush and blotting it off with a bunched-up, dry paper tissue. This is the *wet-and-blot* technique. Note that the light patches are islands of white and the shadows were left untouched from the original wash.

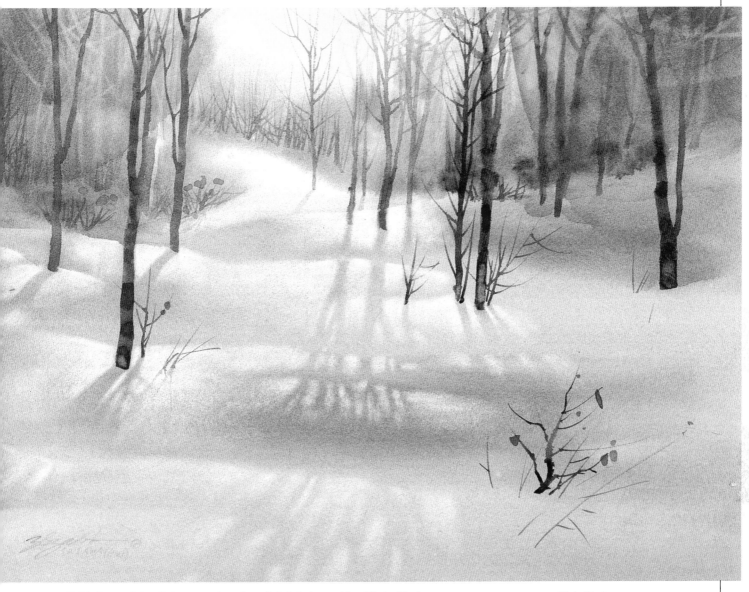

To lift the sunlight off the snow, I used my little bristle scrubber filled with clean water and loosened the pigment in just a small area at a time. I started at the top of the hill where the light is the strongest. I made sure that the shadows stayed intact, lifting out only the islands of light. The edges of the shadows closest to the trees remain sharp, while the shadows extending into the foreground have softer edges and less contrast. Note that all the shadows taper towards the imaginary location of the sun.

Stoic Shadows
35x45.5cm (13¾x18in)
Noblesse cold-pressed paper.
Collection of Willa McNeill.

Sunlight on Snow

Instead of the backlighting seen on the previous two pages, here we see strong frontlighting on snow, sending the shadows away from us. The dark background colour is made by flooding lighter colours into a dark base wash. This must be achieved while the first neutral dark wash is shiny wet. Light colours replace dark colours easily when flooded into very wet paint, but behave unpredictably if the first wash sits too long. Experiment with this effect. The bright foreground is left white except for the cool shadow and lone grasses.

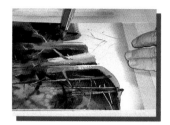

Use a 2.5cm (1in) slant or straight-cut bristle brush for the dark drybrush touches. The brush should be full of very dark colour with very little water. For ideal results don't press the brush too hard or you'll get a lump. Barely touch the surface and the result will be free and lacy.

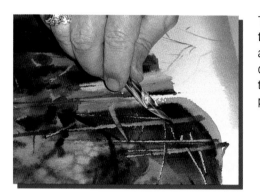

To scrape out the shapes of the light trees, use the oval tip of the brush handle. The colour is applied in a rich consistency and scraped immediately. The brush handle is held firmly between the thumb and fingers, but the wrist delivers the pressure.

Wet-into-wet, warm-dominated colours.

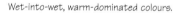

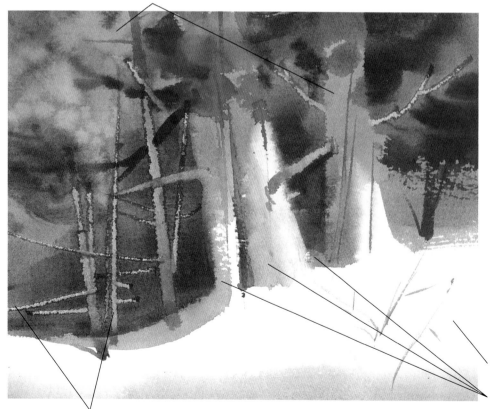

To indicate bright sunlight, I painted the dark background, leaving out the large trees as negative shapes. My colours were cadmium red-orange, rose madder, cyanine blue and phthalo green in various combinations. I did the small tree trunks with the slanted end of a brush handle while the dark wash was still wet. After the first wash was dry, I glazed the shadows onto the tree trunks as well as the little weeds and their shadows.

Untouched white paper.

Cool shadows.

Scraped out of wet background.

Warmly Lit Snow

Painting warm light on a naturally cool subject is an interesting challenge. One technique is first to cover the area with a cool wash, lift off most of it, and then glaze with a warm note. When you glaze a warm colour over a cooler shape that was scrub-lifted, you are working over a slightly damaged surface. Make sure that your paper is bone dry and cover the surface fast with a large, soft brush. Don't go back and forth or the surface may get mottled.

After lifting off shadow colour dominated by manganese blue, gamboge yellow was glazed over the area to reflect the sky colour.

Warm sky colour.

Original shadow colour left after lifting off.

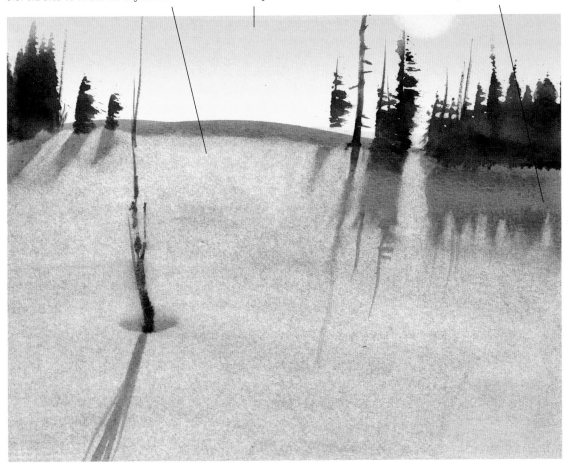

I started with the golden sky, painting the blended wash with a 5cm (2in) soft brush using a mixture of gamboge yellow and rose madder. I painted the whole snowy hill with the same blue colour as the shadows, and let it dry. My shadow colours were manganese blue and some rose madder. While this was drying, I painted in the dark evergreens with my 5cm (2in) slant bristle brush using a strong mix of rose madder, manganese blue and a small amount of phthalo green. I then scrubbed out the large foreground area, leaving the shadows untouched. Because the lifted-off colour was too blue-white for the warm light conditions, I glazed a very thin wash of gamboge yellow over the sunlit snow (shadows included) to warm it up.

Falling Snow

There are various ways to represent falling snow in watercolour. This salt technique is one I like, as long as it is used sparingly. There is only one trap with this technique and it is timing. Sprinkle the salt just as the shine of your wash goes dull; you have about thirty seconds to do it. If you act too soon, the salt will dissolve and create 'uglies'; if you put it on too late, nothing happens. The effect takes about fifteen seconds to start showing. Don't be impatient and throw in more salt – too much is the kiss of death. Again, don't use salt all the time, only when the technique is absolutely called for.

Carefully timed application of salt created these snowflakes.

Dark shapes were painted into an almost dry surface.

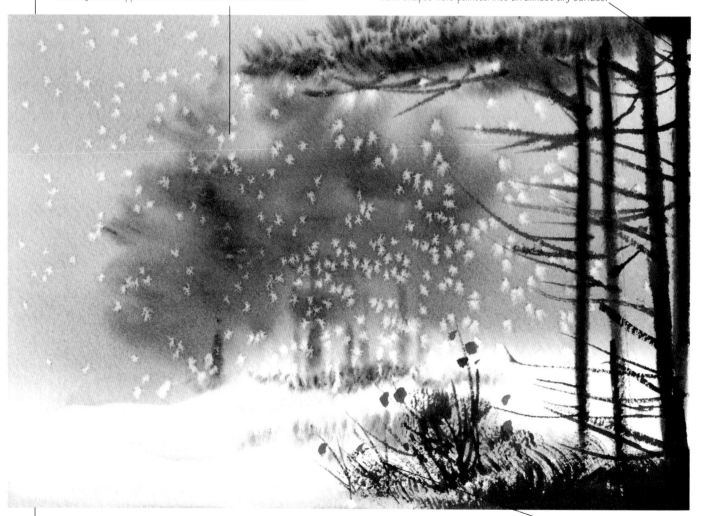

I painted the moody background with burnt sienna, gold ochre and ultramarine blue, using a 2.5cm (1in) bristle brush filled with rich colours and a little water on a wet surface. For the pines I added some phthalo green to the previous dark combination. I sprinkled salt into the wash just before it lost its shine. I used only a few grains of salt; more salt may create an overpowering blizzard effect.

Drybrush strokes were applied after the paper had dried.

Trees in Heavy Snow

I want you to look for two areas of interest in this little colour sketch.
(1) Most of the washes are not only light in tone but clean as well.
Spontaneity is the reason for the smooth clarity of the colours. (2) The
water droplets in the sky must be applied just as the shine of the wash
goes dull. You may have slightly varying results each time, because it is
impossible to match the timing to the split second. Expect the outcome
to be fun, not perfection.

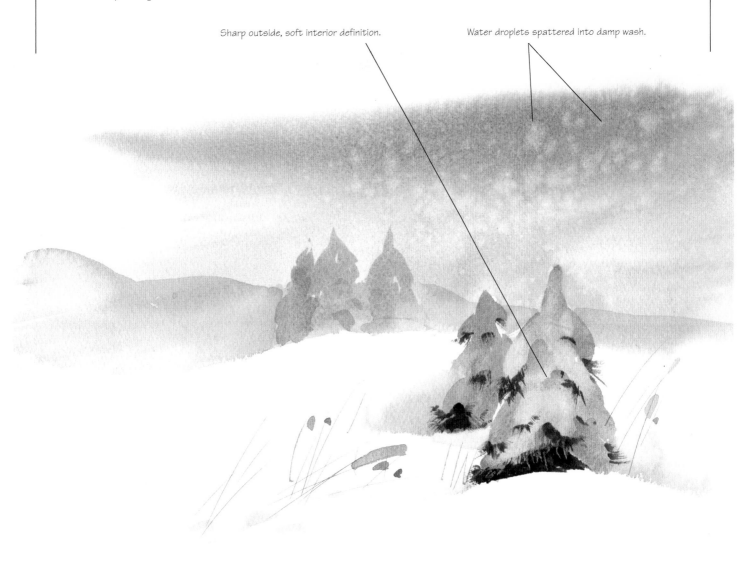

Sharp outside, soft interior definition.

Water droplets spattered into damp wash.

My colours were burnt sienna, cyanine blue and ultramarine blue for the sky. I started with a burnt sienna and ultramarine blue wash on wet paper. I used the bristle
brush to spatter a few water droplets into the drying colour to hint at snowflakes.
Then I painted the silhouette of the snow-covered trees. After the colour dried, I drybrushed the few dark, exposed branches. I used the lost-and-found edge technique
for shading the snow on the trees as well as on the ground.

Young Spruce in Snow

The most important element in this little example is also the most subtle one: shading the snow with lost-and-found edges. Sharp edges read clearer than soft ones. Whatever subject you paint, sooner or later you'll need to paint something that has a sharp edge on one side and a soft edge on the other. Any subject, a portrait, a figure, a landscape or an abstract watercolour, may use this technique.

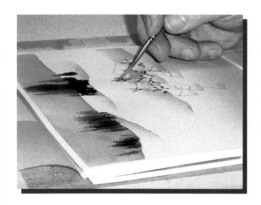

Paint the delicate baby spruce branches sticking out of the snow immediately after dampening the dry paper. Use a No. 3 rigger filled with rich paint and very little water. As soon as the dark colour touches the damp surface, it blurs a little to look like the fine needles of a spruce branch. It is important to apply the colour with a delicate touch and just the right amount of moisture.

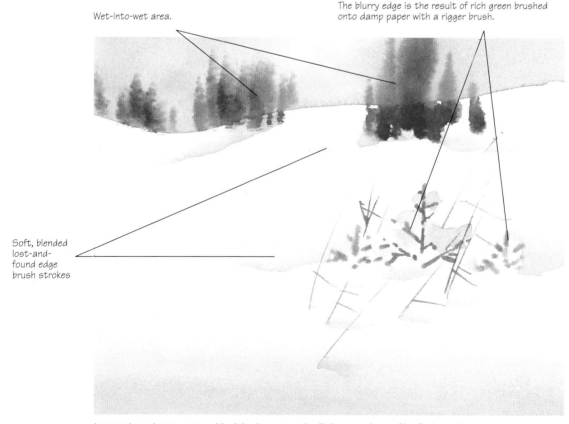

Wet-into-wet area.

The blurry edge is the result of rich green brushed onto damp paper with a rigger brush.

Soft, blended lost-and-found edge brush strokes

I started on damp paper with rich pigment and a little water in my No. 3 rigger to paint the fine spruce branches. I allowed the edges to soften slightly as the brush touched the damp surface. I shaded the snow with lost-and-found edges. My colours were phthalo green and gold ochre for the young spruces and burnt sienna and a little magenta for the snow. I used the cutting edge of the palette knife for the thin weeds. In the background I used the same colours for the sky and the trees.

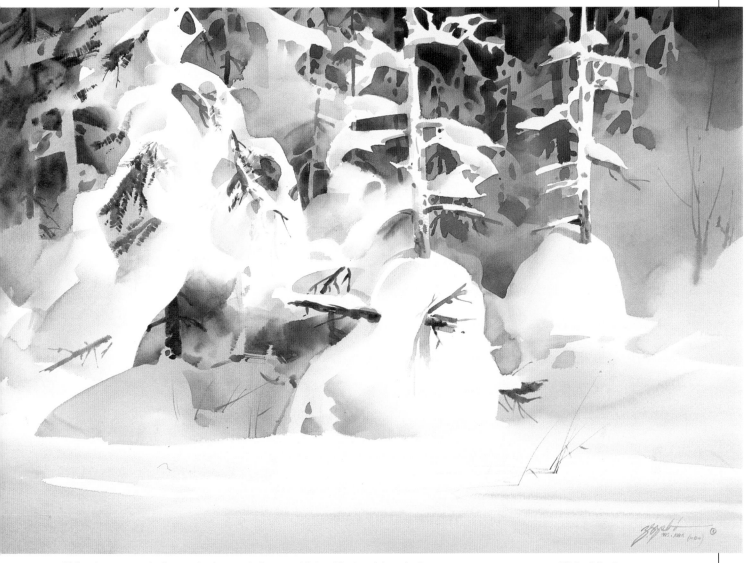

This winter scene is the result of several glazes and lots of lost-and-found edge control in the depiction of the snow. I started with a medium-tone glaze round the white snow. This colour is still visible at the top right edge. As this was drying, I painted the next darkest tone, exposing the silhouette of the shaded trees in the tone of the first wash. The darkest glaze at the top came last, together with the branch structure showing dark accents here and there. I shaded the snow humps by applying the shadow colours and blending away the edges facing the sun. This lost-and-found edge technique enabled me to make the snow look soft, deep and inviting. The reddish bark complements the otherwise cool dominance of the painting.

Winter Friends
38x56cm (15x22in)
Collection of Tom Malone
and Susan Pfahl.

Heavy Fog

Fog can create moody and mysterious visual conditions. While very close objects can be colourful and clear, other objects seem to melt quickly into the atmosphere as they move towards the distance. The shapes behind the fog must be painted first with dominating staining colours like Payne's grey or sepia. If your first wash doesn't stain, it will come off when you glaze the fog on top of it, however gentle you are. For the fog, don't be sparing with the colour. It should be as thick as pouring cream but still definitely liquid. Heavy fog is painted with thicker consistency paint. Mist is painted with runnier paint, but in the same manner (see pages 82–3). When the colour dries, it will regain its luminosity.

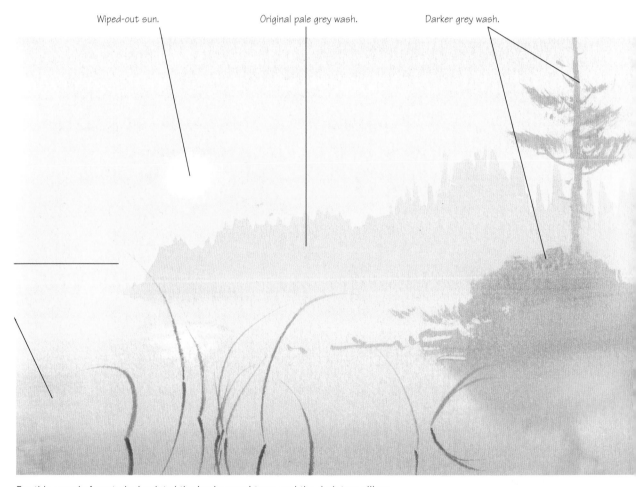

Wiped-out sun.

Original pale grey wash.

Darker grey wash.

Titanium white and cobalt blue glaze.

Titanium white and gold ochre glaze.

For this moody fog study, I painted the background trees and the dark tree silhouette with Vandyke brown and Payne's grey onto my dry paper. When these were dry, I painted a rich reflective wash of cobalt blue, titanium white and gold ochre over the original design using a 6.25cm (2½in) soft brush. Last, for the dark foreground weeds, I used gold ochre and cyanine blue.

Whenever you paint dark colours on top of a dry but opaque wash (as I did in the foreground below), apply the colour quickly to avoid digging up the light colour. With repeated wet brush strokes the colour will actually get lighter. If you need to redo this area because you didn't go dark enough, wait until it dries again and repeat your dark colour on a dry surface.

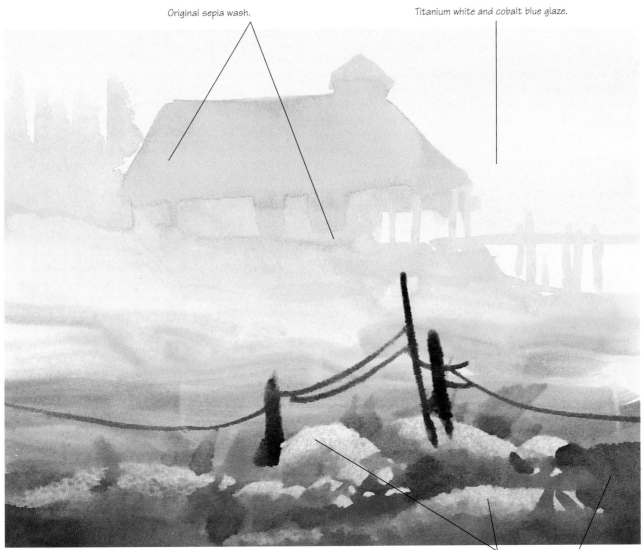

Original sepia wash.

Titanium white and cobalt blue glaze.

Palette knife-scraped light area.

Rocks painted with warm foreground colours.

For the background building and dock, I used a thin wash of Winsor & Newton staining sepia. After it dried, I glazed the fog on top with a mix of titanium white and cobalt blue. My foreground colours, painted last, were Venetian red, Winsor & Newton sepia, cobalt blue and a touch of aureolin yellow for the weeds.

Mist

Even though the wash for the trees was painted with a staining colour (sepia) and allowed to dry, I felt safer applying the blended mist colour over it with a half-loaded large brush, rather than going back and forth many times. When the wet slant brush has paint only in the long-hair end of it and just water in the short hairs, it will blend one side of the brush stroke and leave the other end dark and sharp to read as a strong design element. A straight-cut brush can be used in the same way.

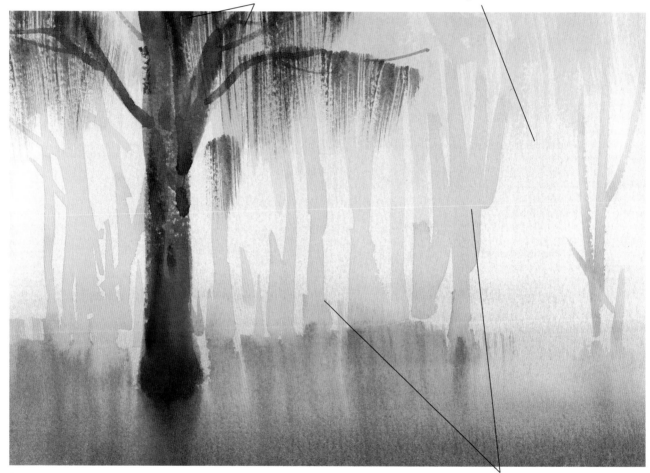

Dark glaze on top of dry mist colour without blending with it.

Cobalt blue and titanium white glaze.

Sepia washes.

On a dry surface, I roughed in a very light wash of the tree trunks in the swamp with Winsor & Newton sepia (a staining colour). After this wash was dry, I glazed on a mix of cobalt blue and a little titanium white with a 6.25cm (2½in) soft brush. This wash was thicker at the top and more diluted near the bottom of the trees. The long-haired end of my brush held the thicker paint and the shorter hairs supplied the water simultaneously. This way the brush stroke blended its own edge as I applied it. Again I let the paint dry completely. The dark tree with the Spanish moss was gently glazed on with a 2cm (¾in) soft flat brush without disturbing the dry mist colour already applied.

For this example I did not use white in the colour mix for glazing the mist. Cobalt blue, a light opaque (reflective) colour, was my choice. Diluting an opaque colour with water is like adding white paint. Water makes watercolour lighter by diluting it. The staining colour of the background wash visually combines with the semi-opaque cobalt wash, showing the translucency of both colours. You can use this technique with any combination of opaque and staining colours on any subject where a soft, misty effect is required. Remember that the strength of the colours is determined by how much water and paint is in your brush.

Graded cobalt blue top glaze.   Sepia under wash.

The silhouette of the building in the background was applied with a faint wash of Winsor & Newton sepia and allowed to dry. I glazed the mist wash over it with a 6.25cm (2½in) soft brush loaded with cobalt blue at its long-haired end but only water in the short hairs. As I repeatedly moved the brush horizontally, the tone of the wash darkened at the top but stayed lighter at the bottom.

Sunlight on Wood

You must use a well sized, high-quality paper for this technique. Noblesse, Arches and Waterford are all papers that will work. For best results, the staining colour used for the wood-grain texture must be the first colour to touch the paper. The less staining the shadow colour is, the easier it is to remove. Test the colours you intend to use on scrap paper before diving into a complex painting.

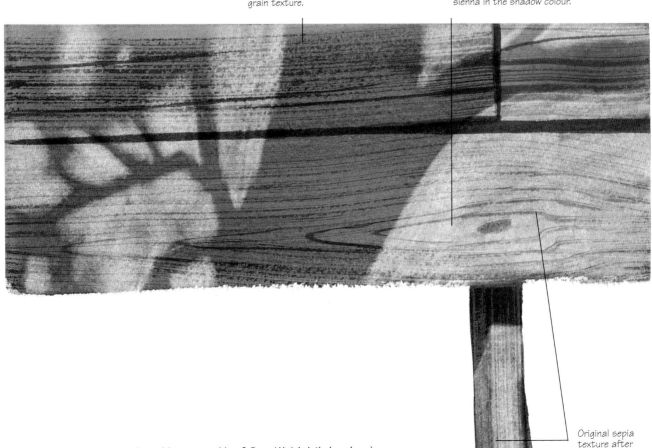

Shadow colour as it dried on top of wood-grain texture.

Slightly stained colour left from burnt sienna in the shadow colour.

Original sepia texture after lifting off shadow colour.

I applied the wood grain on dry, white paper with a 2.5cm (1in) bristle brush using drybrush technique. My colour was Winsor & Newton sepia, a staining colour. After it dried, I glazed a rich but liquid mix of burnt sienna, ultramarine blue and gold ochre over the whole wood surface to represent a shadow tone. I waited for the paper to dry and then lifted out the sunshine areas with a wet-and-blot technique. The wood grain remained unharmed.

Cobweb

This technique works best with a dark background. The moody interior of an old barn or an ancient castle is just the place for a romantic touch such as this. The dark surface shows off the beading, dusty appearance of the cobweb. Be sure your background wash is bone dry. You may want to blow-dry it with a hair dryer for about twenty-five seconds to make sure that any humidity that might have entered the paper from the air is completely removed.

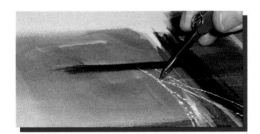

For this effect the paper has to be bone dry. Hold the sharp tip of a small pocket-knife blade firmly between the thumb and fingers at a 90° angle. Pressing very hard, scrape out the beaded lines with several lightning-fast strokes. It is important to use an extremely sharp blade.

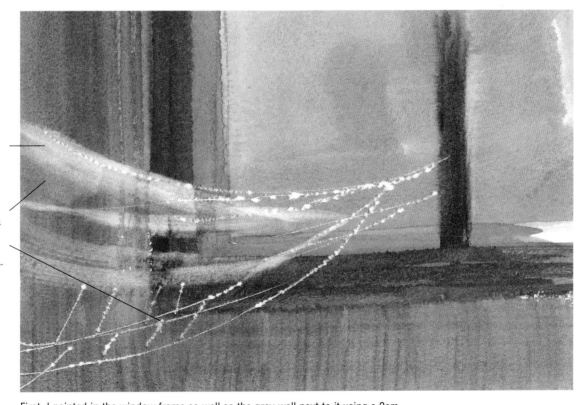

Wet brush used to scrub out dusty, soft web.

Dark background shows the web better.

Scraped out with the sharp tip of a pocket-knife.

First, I painted in the window frame as well as the grey wall next to it using a 2cm (¾in) soft flat brush. I kept these washes on the darkish side with burnt sienna and ultramarine blue. I followed with the outdoor sky colour, cobalt blue, with a little aureolin yellow near the bottom. After everything was dry, I scraped out the thin lines of the web with the very sharp point of my pocket-knife. I held the knife at a very high angle. This way it caught on the paper in a few places, making the impression of a beaded line. I linked several of these lines together to make the web look convincing. To make the web older and dustier looking, I wetted and quickly wiped off some of the colour for the soft, light shapes complementing the white lines.

Simplified Planes

This is an excellent technique for painting on location. A simple hint of texture is all you need. I have simplified these textures by using a glaze (snow on the mountain) and by sandpapering the dry colour (for the shimmer at the bottom edge). Use sandpaper on dried colour to create white shimmer. The edge of a razor blade can be used, and the paper must be bone dry. Don't distract from the simple design.

Keep details, particularly busy texture, out of your mind while using this technique. An exciting silhouette is enough to create strong character for each plane. A uniform tone needs to dominate each plane. Tonal values and colour are the elements used to define the shapes. Texture is a dirty word here.

I started with the light wash in the sky, using a soft, 2cm (¾in) flat brush. After the wash dried, I painted the most distant pale silhouette of the hills. Again I waited for the paper to dry, then dropped in the nearby shore trees in a darker wash. So far my colours were burnt sienna and ultramarine blue. Then I flooded a little aureolin yellow and burnt sienna into this wash on the left side. I glazed in the reflecting water and a few hints of waves at the bottom.

Flooded warm colours.

Natural texture caused by the sedimentary colour settling in the low spots of the paper.

Drybrush indicating shimmer.

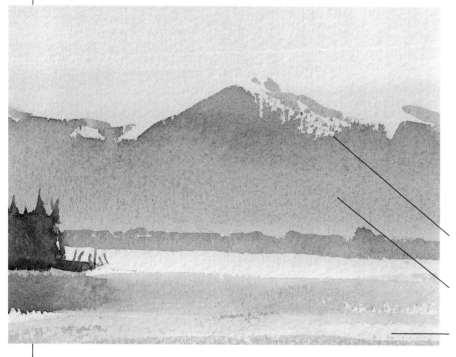

This little sketch was done with only two colours: ultramarine blue and burnt sienna. I proceeded with the wash of the high mountain range using a soft, 2cm (¾in) flat brush fast enough at the top of the wash to skip here and there, creating the illusion of snow. After this wash dried, I painted the medium-dark strip at the white edge of the river, then the darkest and closest group of trees on the left-hand side as well as the reflecting patterns.

Drybrush indicating snow (negative shape).

Graded wash suggesting mist.

Sandpapered light texture.

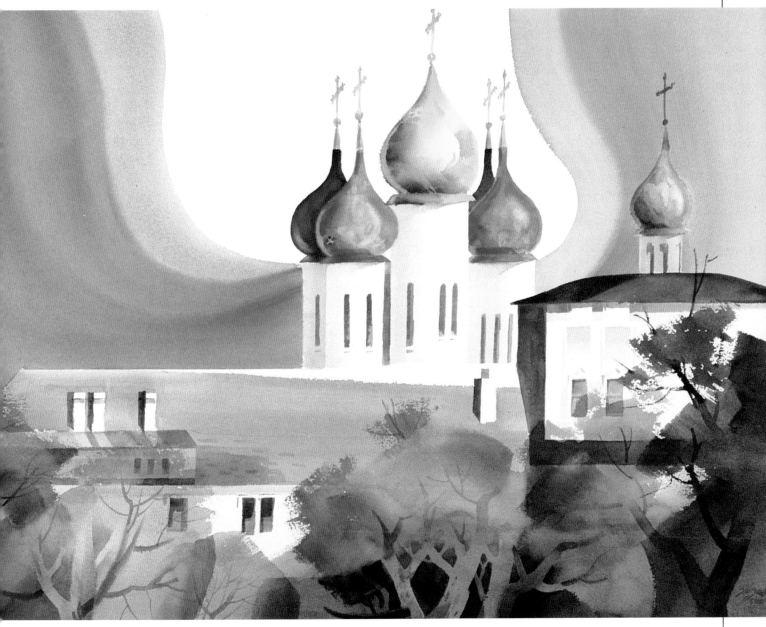

My visit to Russia left a profound impression on me. I was particularly awed by the spiritual qualities of their churches. To communicate this feeling, I repeated the shapes of the onion domes in the background with the colour of the sky. I painted the steeples into the white shape left untouched as a contrasting complement. I treated the buildings as if they were behind the foliage of the trees. The translucent foliage allowed a few building details to come through, and the dark foreground leads the viewer to the light background and the contrasting energy of the powerful focal point – the domes.

New Spirit
56x76cm (22x30in)

Background Forest

This technique can be used for many background situations. Its success depends on decisiveness. Choose colours that can start off the shape with a very wet, neutral colour, establishing the shape's tone. Into this wet wash, flood brighter, lighter colours and let the colours mingle freely. *Don't help them!* The fresh result is your reward for this discipline.

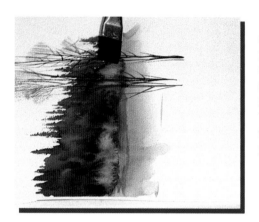

It takes a practised sense of timing to create this effect. With the corner of a 2cm (¾in) flat brush, place a few droplets of water into the drying but still moist dark background colour. The free shapes of the resulting back runs create exciting light impressions that look like frosty shrubs. There's about a 30-second time window, just as the drying paper loses its shine, when this technique works. Bad timing gives a bad outcome.

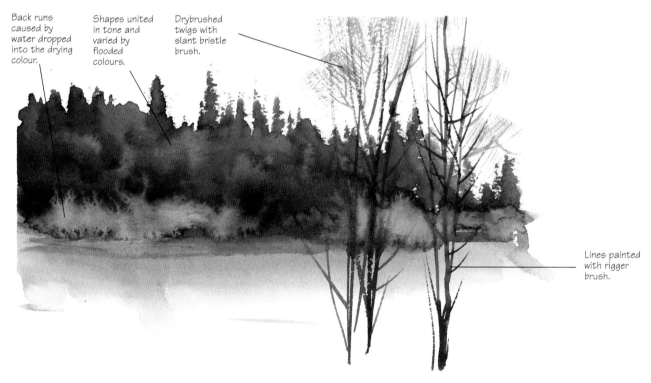

Back runs caused by water dropped into the drying colour.

Shapes united in tone and varied by flooded colours.

Drybrushed twigs with slant bristle brush.

Lines painted with rigger brush.

For this study I used magenta, cyanine blue and cadmium red-orange. I painted the forest shape with a 1.25cm (1½in) bristle brush, aggressively changing colour dominance, dipping into my palette, as I expanded my wash from left to right. I allowed the left side to remain darker and bluer, turning lighter and warmer on the right. Before the colour dried, I placed a few droplets of water at the bottom edge of the wash to indicate frosty shrubs. I also painted in the light blue to indicate icy snow. Total time to this point was about two minutes. After most things were dry, using my rigger I painted the tall trees in the foreground.

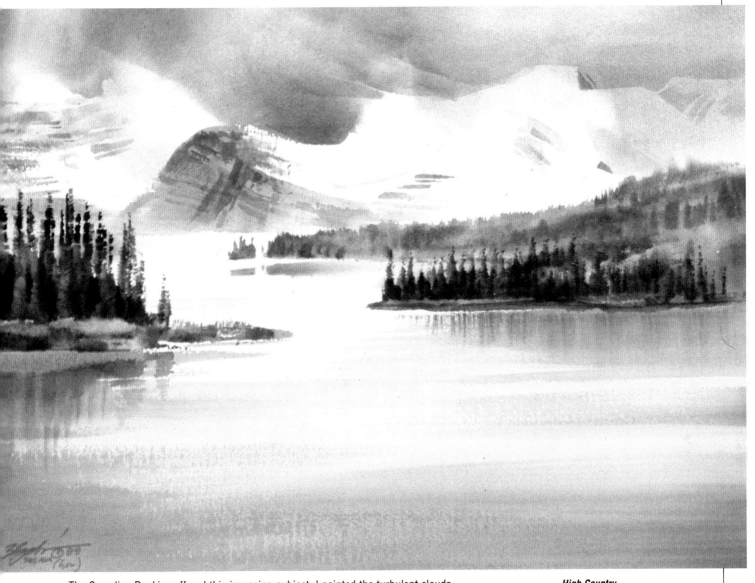

The Canadian Rockies offered this imposing subject. I painted the turbulent clouds wrestling with the snow-covered mountains in the background fast enough to allow some of the washes to wet-blend as they touched. The bright light in the distance is the justification to paint the mountains in warm colours. The middle-ground trees are dominated by dark tones. I painted them with the edge of my slant bristle brush held upright. The water in front is a medium tone and turquoise in colour, typical of silt-influenced lakes of the Rockies. I painted the breezy surface with horizontal brush strokes fast enough to blend, but here and there a little drybrush was incorporated into the active water surface.

High Country
37x51cm (14½x20in)

Winter Island

Evergreens look exciting when painted with this technique. Use the flat side of a slant or straight-cut bristle brush then barely touch the dry paper to get the 'needle' effect. Too much pressure creates a lump that is not as interesting. Don't hesitate or fiddle, just touch down and go.

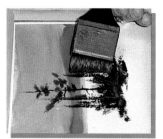

In one stroke you can paint the tapered point of the trees on the wet portion of the background as well as lacy drybrush indicating open foliage over the dry white area. Use a 3.75cm (1½in) bristle brush loaded with dark colour and held at about a 45° angle as you lightly touch the paper, in this way creating the tall evergreen shapes.

Drybrushed with the side of a bristle brush.

Rich colour applied to damp surface with the brush.

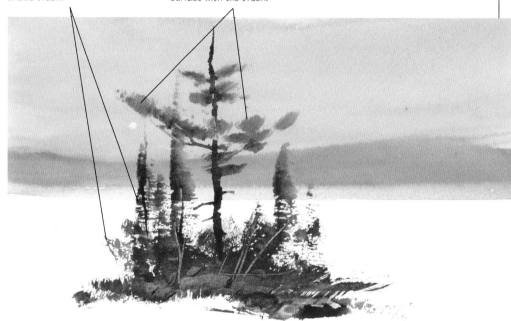

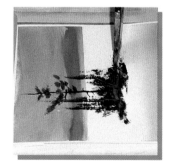

For the lower foliage, hold the edge of the brush sideways and on a vertical angle.

I masked out the distant shore with masking tape, then painted the deep sky and the darker background hills using phthalo green and magenta. After removing the tape, I painted the graded wash at the base with the same colours in light tone using a 5cm (2in) soft slant brush held long-hair end down so the top edge was lost. With a very dark combination of phthalo green, magenta and cadmium red-orange, I pressed my slant bristle brush very gently to form the lacy drybrush where the white paper was bone dry (a straight-cut brush can be used in the same way). The same colour softened against the still-moist background. I played with the bottom edge of the island, heavily pressing my brush to release the dark colours in varying colour dominance. While still moist, I knifed out a few lighter rock and weed shapes.

Rolling Snowbanks

If there is a single brush stroke in watercolour that could be considered the most important, it's the lost-and-found edge. This tricky little fellow can be used on virtually any subject. The sharp edge of the stroke or shape represents dry-paper technique, while the blended edge belongs to the wet-in-wet technique. Practise this brush stroke until you have it under control.

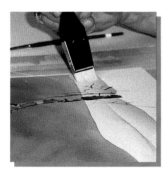

Apply a wet blue brush stroke with a 2cm (¾in) flat, soft brush. To lose the top edge of the bottom light blue brush stroke, touch the colour with the end of a thirsty 2.5cm (1in) brush. This soaks up some of the colour as it moves sideways. Hold the brush at a 45° angle and press it just hard enough to bend the hairs somewhat.

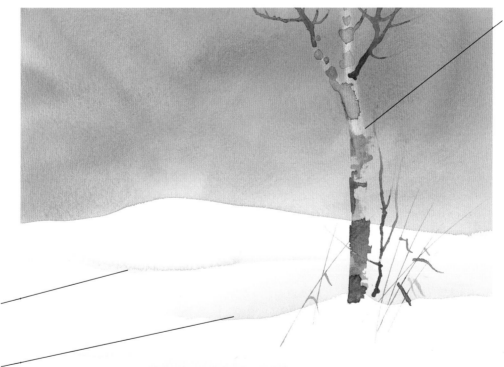

Wet-lifted colour after background had dried.

Back run where too much water was applied.

Lost-and-found edge strokes blended on top to emphasize sharp white at the bottom.

Wherever you see a dip in the snow, the front (bottom) edge of the stroke is sharp, defining the white high spot of the snowbank in front of it. I applied the wash on dry paper (to get a sharp edge) with a soft, flat 2cm (¾in) brush. Immediately I switched to a barely moist 2.5cm (1in) bristle brush and blended the top side. The brush needs to moisten the paper next to the brush stroke and soak up some of the colour simultaneously, allowing the remaining paint to spread into the moist area and to disappear into nothing. Just below the high snowbank at the horizon is a dip where I used too much water in my blending brush and a hard back run happened.

ce on Trees

Timing is very important for this little exercise. Just as the dark background wash loses its shine, go as fast as you can with a little water in your small rigger and paint the frosty branches. (Think of the general shape of the trees, not the branches.) You have only about twenty-five seconds to paint the frosty branches on a sketch like this one. Poking at it after the paint has dried won't help you. Catch it fast when the time is right, then walk away.

Dark background painted onto wet surface.

Clear water stroked into damp colour.

Green charged into wet grey wash.

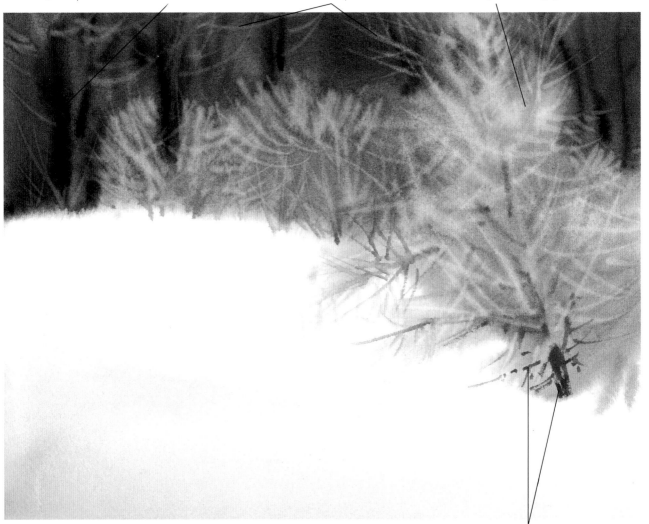

Darks painted after background has dried.

I painted the dark background onto a wet surface using magenta and phthalo green, which promptly neutralized each other. As the wash began to lose its shine, I painted in the ice-covered branches. I used my small rigger and applied clear water in a fast repetitive way, creating rhythmical branch shapes. In the lower right, where the branches reach the white snow, I switched to a little of the combined colours in my rigger and continued painting the pale grey frosty branches against the still-moist white background. After the paper dried, I slipped in the few sharper dark branches at the base of the closest tree.

Frost on Trees

Controlled back runs are a very effective but seldom used extension of the wet-into-wet watercolour painting style. Use them to loosen up your paintings. Feeling is your only guide for these very free shapes. The fast application and the timing are so crucial that you watch the evolution of the tree shapes while you build the back runs with water droplets.

Back runs formed by clear water dropped into drying damp wash.

Dark lines painted into wet wash.

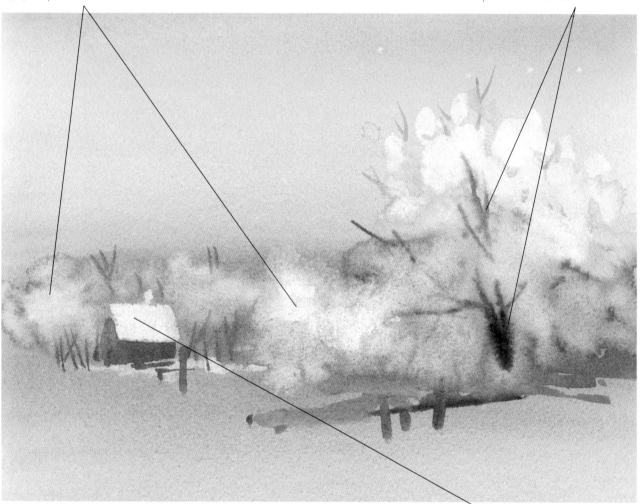

Lifted-out white shape

I chose cerulean blue, ultramarine blue, gold ochre and burnt sienna for this study. I painted the whole surface on wet paper starting at the top with cerulean blue. I continued by adding a little gold ochre to the lower sky and followed with a heavy wash of ultramarine blue and burnt sienna, blended a bit lighter as I spread the wash downwards to the bottom edge of the paper. After about a minute, the wash started to dry, so I dribbled little droplets of clear water with my rigger, creating the frosty-looking back runs. I also painted a few tree trunks, branches, and the distant log cabin into the almost-dry shapes to give the scene a little sense of reality. I removed the white snow on the roof with the wet-and-blot technique after everything had dried.

Setting Sun

When painting a sunset (or a sunrise) remember that nothing can be lighter than the light source – the sun. The trickiest parts of the sketch below are the hot-colour flooded washes in the tree trunks near the bright sun. The dark, cool wash of the tree must be flooded with a warm colour while it is wet. Cadmium orange is the hottest colour in this sketch. The flooded colour is applied generously to look right even after the colour dries. Keep the hue and tones consistent.

Dark foliage drybrushed onto dry surface.

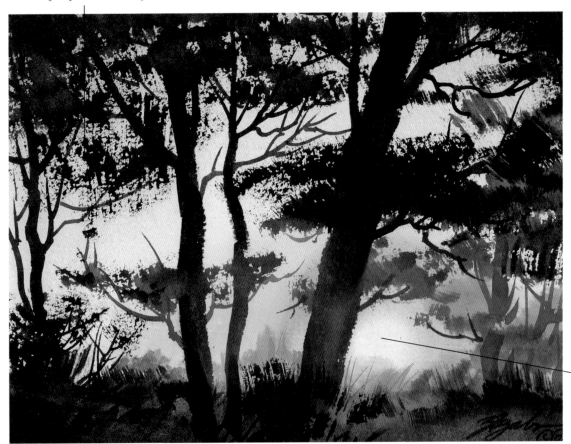

Wet-lifted sun.

I started this sketch by painting the background onto a wet surface. I began with ultramarine blue at the top. I moved my 2.5cm (1in) soft brush with a curving motion around the sun's circular shape. Where the sun is located, I dropped in a heavy splash of gamboge yellow and surrounded it with glowing cadmium red-orange. All these washes blended into each other. The warm, dark foreground came from a mix of phthalo green, rose madder and a bit of cadmium red-orange. As the colour was drying, I lifted out much of the gamboge yellow and the light colour of the sun resulted. My lightest tone was established. After the paper dried, I applied the very dark silhouette of the trees' foliage with the flat side of a heavily loaded 5cm (2in) bristle brush, lightly touching the dry paper. I flooded the wet washes near the sun, as well as the reddish-brown middle-ground trees on the right side, with a lot of cadmium red-orange. The result is hot colour dominance and very high tonal contrast.

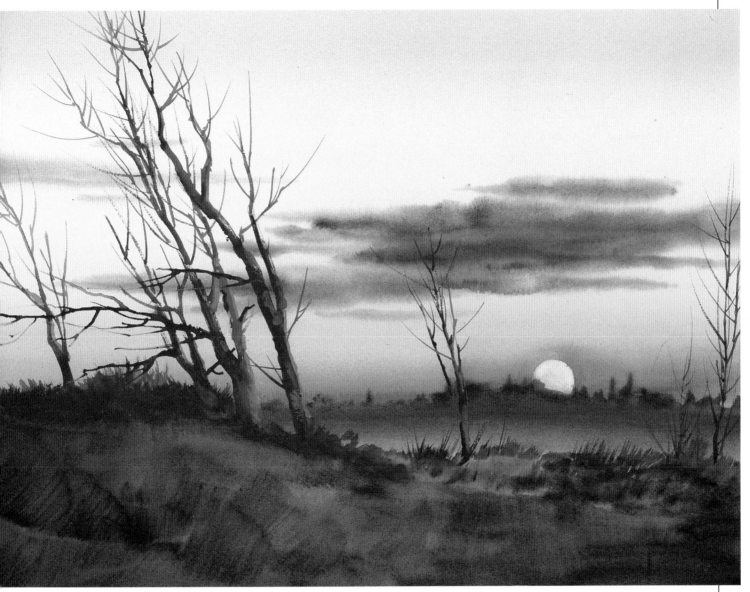

Close to where I planned the sun's location, I flooded the dark, wet foreground wash with cadmium lemon, cadmium orange and some magenta to echo the powerful light of my light source. When that was dry, I masked out a circle shape, and with the 2.5cm (1in) brush loaded with clear water, I scrubbed off the colour and blotted it into a paper tissue, exposing the light shape of the sun. Because the colour looked a little too white, I tinted it with a bit of warm yellow colour.

The Last Wink
35x45.5cm (13¾x18in)
Noblesse cold-pressed paper.
Collection of Ruth and
Jack Richeson.

Negative Shapes

Negative shapes are the shapes that are left after we paint round them. Negative shapes stay white if the paper is white. If the surface has a light colour on it, the negative shape will show that colour. The background *next to* the negative shape is actively painted and the light shape is left out. The colour that defines the negative shape must be darker than the shape it surrounds. A good rule is to think of the negative shape's design while you are painting the positive brush strokes.

Flooded colours with drybrush.

Negative shapes defined by dark wash next to them.

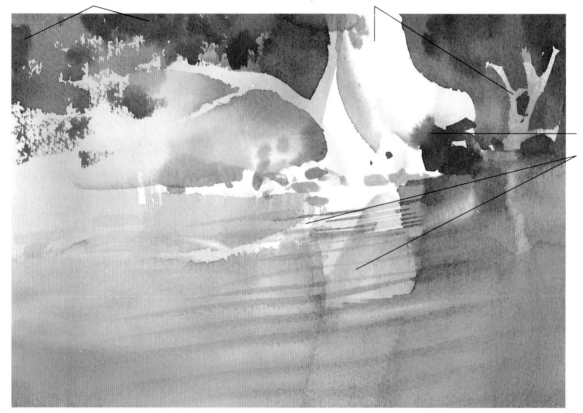

Isolated colour attracts the eye.

Reflection of negative shapes.

To give the white tree a sharp edge, I painted the background and the water simultaneously around the shape of the tree and its reflection. My wet washes were highly charged with different dominant colours. I used a 3.75cm (1½in) soft brush with cadmium red-orange, magenta and gamboge yellow. I glazed the ripples after the wash of the water had dried. The isolated burst of cadmium red-orange next to the white tree attracts extra attention to the centre of interest.

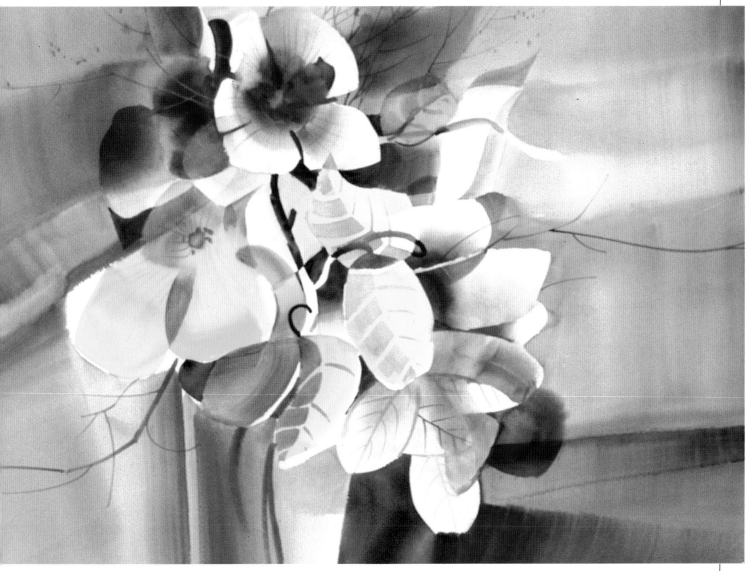

This stylized flower impression is an expression of bouncy colours complemented by a calmer and more neutral background. I first established the approximate colours and shapes of the group of flowers. I treated them as curvilinear negative shapes while I painted the background around them. I allowed the background shapes to blend softly as they touched. I also took advantage of the staining nature of cyanine blue and separated the other colours from it, exposing an occasional clear blue stain. One of these is clearly visible in the background to the left of the yellow petals and at the bottom centre to the right of the white petal. The happy colour impression suggested the title.

Birthday Wish
56x76cm (22x30in)

Flooded Washes

For this approach, your silhouette colour (here, indicating a church) establishes the tone of the shape. You must apply the flooded colours, particularly when light pigments are replacing dark ones, with lots of water and paint in your brush and on the paper. You may have to repeat the flooding four or five times, so use very rich, liquid colour each time you touch the wash. Remember – everything must be dripping wet.

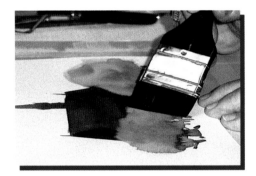

As soon as the dark silhouette of the building is painted, flood the still very wet wash with a very wet brush full of yellow pigment. Repeat this move several times, wiping the brush clean with a tissue between each application. When the dark colour is completely replaced by the yellow, let all the colours dry.

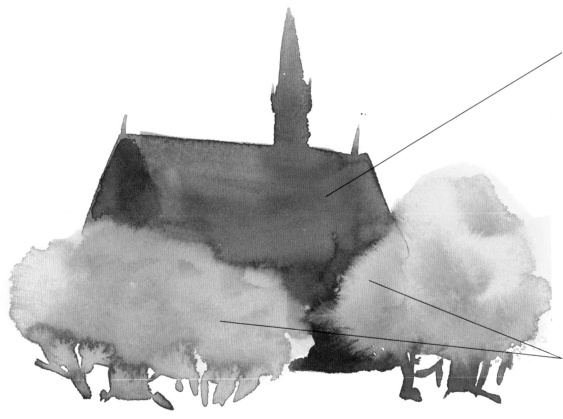

Neutral dark shape was flooded with bright, cleaner pigments.

Full brush of wet, bright yellow flooded into dark, wet background colour.

I started with a dark neutral silhouette of the building's shape. My colours were phthalo green, magenta and gamboge yellow. While this shape was very wet, I flooded in the bright yellow trees, removing the dark corners of the building and replacing them with the yellow hue. Even a dark staining colour, freshly applied and wet, can be replaced by another strong, wet mixture with a few repeated applications. The yellow foliage was also flooded with a little magenta.

Colourful Darks

Dark washes tend to be boring if they are colourless. To make them more interesting, flood them with other colours. Keep the tonal range of the flooded colours close enough to the original wash in order not to change the light condition drastically. Remember, this is a wet technique. Both the wash and the flooded colour in your brush must be very wet.

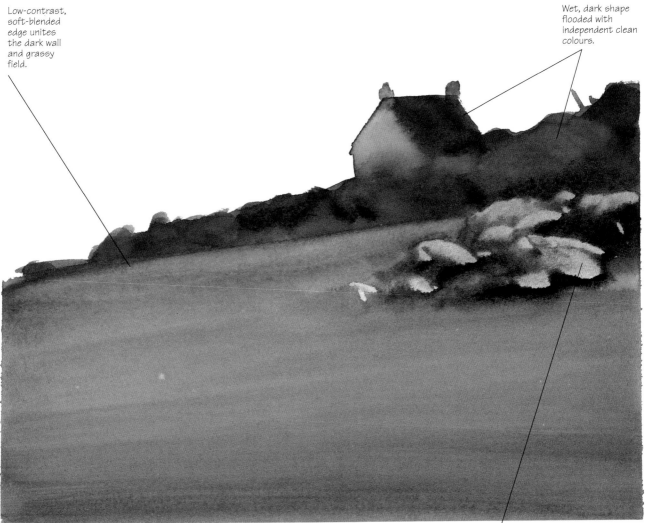

Low-contrast, soft-blended edge unites the dark wall and grassy field.

Wet, dark shape flooded with independent clean colours.

Light shapes lifted from wet surface with a palette knife.

This simple hillside study is painted with phthalo green, rose madder, magenta and gamboge yellow. I started by painting the shape of the house and foliage in a medium tone mixed out of all four colours, using a 2cm (¾in) soft flat brush. While this wash was still wet, I flooded individual colours into the wash, allowing them to dominate local areas. Next, I painted the green hillside, dominating the mixture with gamboge yellow. Before the paper was dry, I dropped in the dark background colour for the rock pile and knifed out the light top of the rocks with the heavily pressed heel of the palette knife. The uninterrupted medium and dark tones suggest a strong unity in the sketch.

Smooth Tree Bark

Here are some more opportunities to use your palette knife, but for this technique to work properly, don't paint your colour too wet. The wash must be tacky and barely moist as you apply it. The knifing must take place immediately, particularly for the fine texture. If the colour is too wet, it will stain the paper by the time it dries enough to be in a workable condition, and it will look messy. Further, if you knife the colour while it's too wet, the knife stroke will actually go dark because the wet paint will creep back into the knifed area. Do it right the first time – apply your colour with very little water.

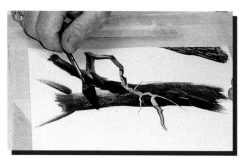

To achieve the bark texture, scrape off the damp colour, holding the palette knife firmly by the handle. The thumb transfers the necessary pressure from the wrist. The scraping edge of the knife is held at a 35° angle and pressed a little harder at the widest part, creating the lightest lifted tone. As you lift the blade towards its point, the gradually reduced pressure results in the bark texture as the tone changes.

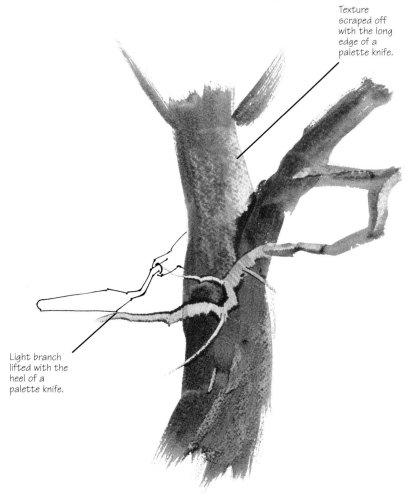

Texture scraped off with the long edge of a palette knife.

Light branch lifted with the heel of a palette knife.

I started this study by painting the shape of the tree trunk with a 3.75cm (1½in) slant bristle brush filled with a rich consistency of Winsor & Newton sepia. As soon as I put my brush down, I lifted out the texture with my palette knife. I held it pointing to the left, with the edge of the knife pressing hard at the wide part (heel) and releasing the pressure towards the tip. I moved the knife downwards and the texture you see is the result. While the colour was still wet, I painted the limbs. Where the curving branch bends in front of the trunk, I extended the shape by knifing out the light branch, pressing hard on the heel of the knife.

Rough Tree Bark

To create this texture, the base colour must feel tacky, not too wet. The knife doesn't need to be pressed too hard if the consistency of your colour is right. If the wash is too wet, the knife strokes will go dark as the watery wash gushes back into them. Be confident when you press the knife's heel, though great pressure is not required. Remember you are painting sharp, light shapes into a damp colour. The condition of your wash must be just right.

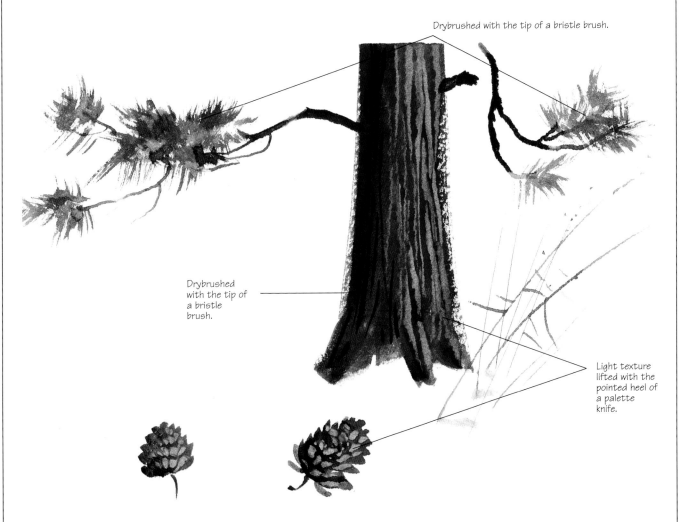

Drybrushed with the tip of a bristle brush.

Drybrushed with the tip of a bristle brush.

Light texture lifted with the pointed heel of a palette knife.

This rough bark texture started with a quickly applied shape brushed on with a 3.75cm (1½in) bristle brush. My colours were burnt sienna and phthalo blue. Just as soon as I was finished and while the colour was still fresh, I knifed off the light texture by stroking back and forth with the heel of my palette knife. I moved the knife up and down, tilting the blade back and forth as if I were sharpening a straight razor on a leather strap.

My technique was similar on the pine cones but I used short, repetitive strokes for the light shapes.

I drybrushed the foliage clusters with the tip of my bristle brush in the direction the needles grow.

Glazed Tree Bark

Here, the neutral tree trunk shape is painted with semi-complementary colours that make it less monotonous. The colours flood the grey wash and add a colourful influence. For this approach to be truly effective, the wet-into-wet technique must be used.

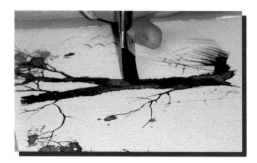

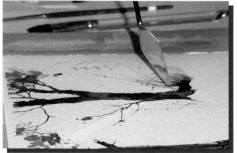

For the relatively small shape of this tree, apply the flooded colours with a 2cm (¾in) flat, soft brush. Use the corner of the brush with gentle pressure to drop the pure colours into the wet shape of the tree. Timing is crucial. Act while the first wash is still very wet.

For the delicate weeds, hold the palette knife upright and cut a line into the paper, pressing the tip and releasing a small amount of wet colour into the groove simultaneously. The high angle is important to allow gravity to help in freeing the wet colour.

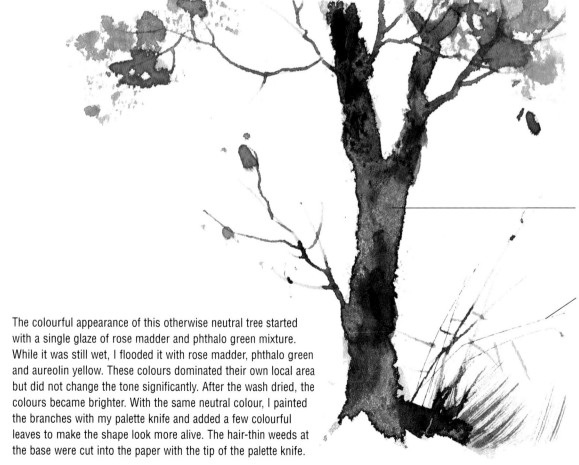

Dark grey flooded with yellow, red and green.

Line done with the sharp tip of a palette knife.

The colourful appearance of this otherwise neutral tree started with a single glaze of rose madder and phthalo green mixture. While it was still wet, I flooded it with rose madder, phthalo green and aureolin yellow. These colours dominated their own local area but did not change the tone significantly. After the wash dried, the colours became brighter. With the same neutral colour, I painted the branches with my palette knife and added a few colourful leaves to make the shape look more alive. The hair-thin weeds at the base were cut into the paper with the tip of the palette knife.

Tree Impressions

With the same brush stroke you can make very different tree impressions depending on whether the paper is wet or dry. The clear water approach requires dark, wet colours and very careful timing to hit the paint just as it loses its shine. On dry paper, apply your brush strokes with very light pressure. The weight of the brush is almost enough. On a wet medium- to dark-tone wash, brush the damp paper with a small, flat bristle brush or scrape with a brush handle.

Strokes painted with bristle brush on a wet surface.

Clear water applied into damp colour.

Strokes painted with bristle brush on dry paper surface.

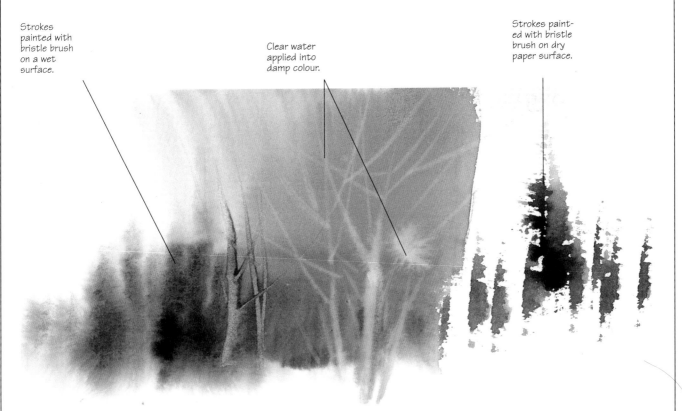

Clear Water

Using cyanine blue and Winsor & Newton sepia, I painted a hint of a forest-like setting on wet paper with a 5cm (2in) bristle brush. The brush was not too wet, and it soaked up water and deposited the colours simultaneously.

Wet Wash

Just after the drying colour lost its shine, I brushed in the shape of the light tree fast enough to keep the spreading light shape from running out of control. At the dark section of the background, I removed the light tree shapes with the tip of my slanted plastic brush handle.

Dry Paper

On dry paper I held the 5cm (2in) bristle brush flat so that the handle was parallel with the paper and the narrow end was at the top of the evergreen. The edge of the hair was lined up with the potential location of the tree trunk. As I touched the paper, half of the evergreen shape emerged. To do the other half, I flipped the brush to its other side and repeated the stroke.

Rock Setting

A very important part of this technique is to flood the otherwise dark base wash with pure staining colours. These will stain the paper, and after you knife out the shapes of the rocks, they will show these dominant hues in a lighter tone, making them sparkle with colour. Staining colours are the key here. (Staining colours are discussed on page 20.)

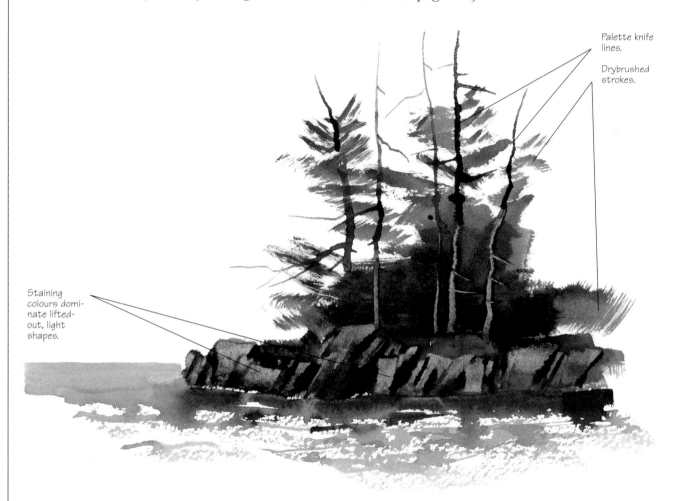

Palette knife lines.

Drybrushed strokes.

Staining colours dominate lifted-out, light shapes.

First, I painted the foliage of the pine clump using rose madder, burnt sienna, cyanine blue and phthalo green in varied dominance. From this very dark, wet shape, I knifed out the light tree trunks and branches. Then I painted the dark part of the tree trunks with a small rigger. To paint the rocky foreground, I added dark colours strongly dominated by individual hues at different areas. With the firm heel of my palette knife, I squeezed off the slab-like shapes of the rocks. The colour dominance became even more evident in these lighter shapes. I glazed the water, drybrushing the lower edge to hint of sparkling waves.

Palette Knife Trees

You must use very liquid paint for this technique. The paint must flow off the knife the same way it flows out of a brush. When you paint the branches, hold the knife lightly and drag it with a light pressure against its tip, without lifting it, until it runs out of paint. This technique can also be used for exciting abstract background texture, particularly if you crisscross your shapes or apply different colours for different strokes. Don't limit this or any other technique to only one subject. Expand on it by using your imagination.

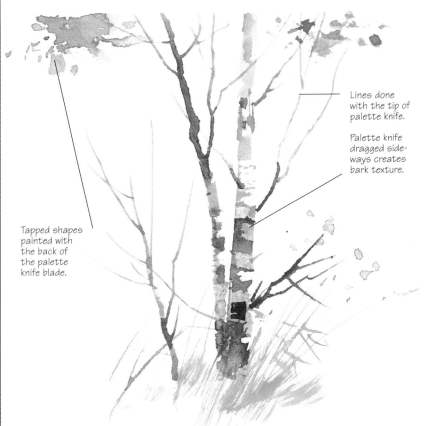

Lines done with the tip of palette knife.

Palette knife dragged sideways creates bark texture.

Tapped shapes painted with the back of the palette knife blade.

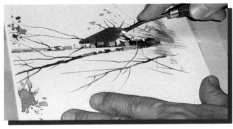

For the loose birch bark effect, dip the palette knife in wet colour, and holding it at a low angle, touch the edge on the dry paper and make a horizontal dragging stroke. Where the colour comes off as a solid wet shape, knife off the light sections immediately with the firmly pressed heel of the blade. The knife's response is unpredictable; be prepared to add or remove colour as required.

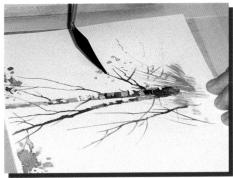

My colours were cyanine blue, rose madder and aureolin yellow. I painted these trees entirely with my palette knife. For the trunk I used a little liquid paint on my knife's edge, and touching it to the paper, dragged it from one side of the trunk to the other. Where the colour is textured, I left it alone. Where it was too solid, I knifed out a lighter strip. I repeated this, varying my colours a little. With a dark liquid mix on the palette knife, I painted the branches and the young sapling. I even tapped on a few leaves with the back of my knife point. 'Tapping' is touching the paper repeatedly with the back of the knife blade, to which the liquid paint is applied. The delicate, tall weeds were cut into the paper with the edge of the knife tip covered with a little liquid paint. The small, drybrushed grass cluster at the tree's base was the only part done with a brush.

The position and angle of the palette knife is important as you paint the branches. The liquid paint rushes off the blade if it is held at a very high angle, while its flow slows down if the blade is held flatter. Drag the knife's tip away from the trunk to allow the branches to taper towards their point.

Brush-Handle Trees

For this technique, use a brush that has a slanted tip at the end of the handle. For a larger painting, try using some other firm tool, such as a credit card. The important thing is to watch the condition of your wet colour: don't use it too wet or too dry. If you use a 640gsm (300lb) paper for a larger painting, it will stay moist a little longer, giving you additional time to manoeuvre a little more complex design with this lifting-out method. For narrow shapes, I still recommend the use of the slanted tip of a plastic brush handle.

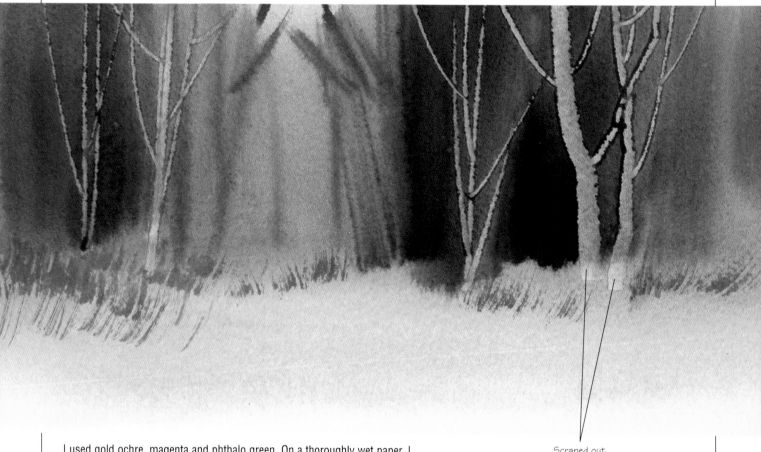

Scraped out from a damp colour with the tip of the slanted end of a plastic brush handle.

I used gold ochre, magenta and phthalo green. On a thoroughly wet paper, I brushed in the tone and silhouette of the forest with a 5cm (2in) bristle brush filled with lots of paint and just a little water. Where individual dark trees appear, I used only the tip of the brush. When I stopped painting, the paper was barely moist and just right for scraping out the light trees. I held the tip of my plastic brush handle slightly sideways for the widest tree. Then with very firm pressure I scraped off the colour. Even movement was essential for a successful shape. For the thinner branches, I held the brush handle on a higher angle. Because the ideally moist condition doesn't last long, timing is crucial. This scraping, for example, took only a few seconds. The drybrush grasses were applied for variety.

Soft Lifted-out Trees

This technique is a lot of fun. The ideal condition of the paper is between very wet and dry. For the dark, soft shapes use much less water in the brush than there is on the paper. For the light shapes, a controlled, small amount of clear water in your small brush painted into the damp colour brings a very exciting result. If you should be a little late and the water is not spreading, let it sit for a half a minute and loosen the pigment. Then blot it by pressing a tissue over the shape. The chances are that you will get your light lines anyway.

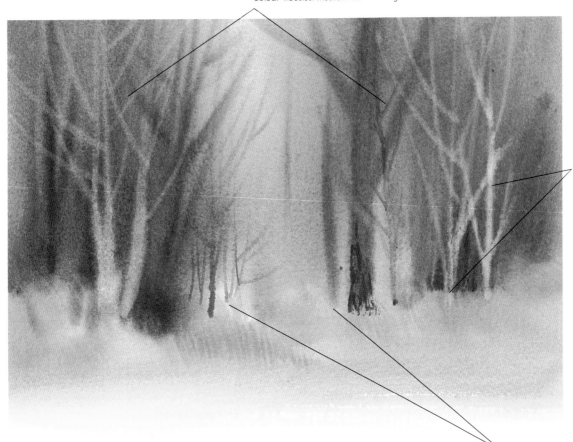

Colour-flooded medium-dark background.

Clear water strokes painted into drying damp background.

Dark lines painted into damp colour.

After I had wet the paper completely, I painted the dark tones of the forest with a rich mix of burnt sienna and cobalt blue. When the larger shapes looked good, I painted the ground with a gold-ochre dominance in a rich wash made from all three colours. At this point I mixed a very dark combination of burnt sienna and cobalt blue, dominated by burnt sienna, and painted the darker trees with the tip of the brush. As the wash was losing its shine, I lifted out the wide lighter tree with a 2cm (¾in) flat brush in a damp but thirsty condition. Then I switched to a No. 5 rigger and defined the light trees and branches by introducing a little water from the tip of my rapidly moving brush. Because the wet condition held, I sketched in the blurry but clearly readable young trees in the centre region with a rich mixture of blue-grey in my rigger.

Wet-into-Wet Evergreens

Wet-into-wet watercolour is a technique so versatile it can be used on any paper with any tool and with any brand of watercolour, but you must keep an important point in mind to succeed with it easily. However wet your paper is, always keep less water in your brush than there is on the paper. When they touch, the water unites. Too much water in your brush, and you've got a gushing back run. Not enough, and you have a lump or a smear. A firm bristle brush has just the right temperament for wet-into-wet painting. If you need to reduce water in your brush, blot it on a paper pad.

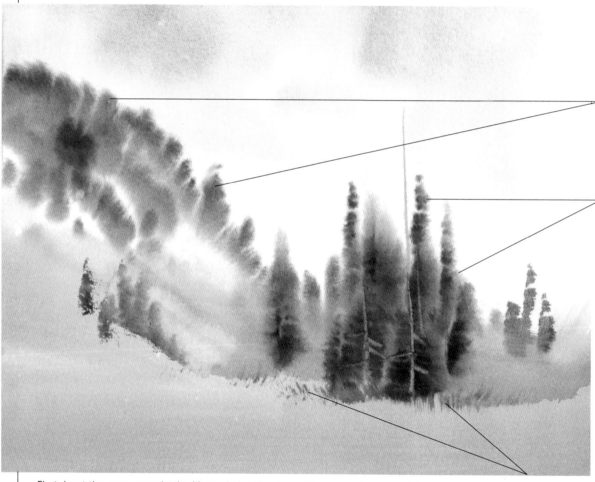

Repeated dark brush strokes on very wet paper.

These warm, dark shapes are painted on wet paper with the edge of a bristle brush.

Dry brush strokes on dry surface.

First, I wet the paper completely. After painting the sky and the snowy foreground, I painted the background trees in a curving line indicating a hill. For these rapidly applied, rhythmical shapes, I used the corner of my 5cm (2in) bristle brush, heavily loaded with a rich mix of burnt sienna and cobalt blue. The moisture on the surface blurred the shapes into a soft, drifting mood. Then without picking up any more water, I filled my brush with darker colour and firmly touched the wet surface with the edge of the brush. As the surface was drying, I finished by scraping out a few light tree trunks and branches.

Sunlit Mountain Tops

Just a little warning. When you paint subjects like this one where the colour needs to be flawlessly clean, use a very clean brush, fresh colour and also unpolluted mixing water. Dirt in any of them can jeopardize the necessary brilliance of the colours. The drama is the result of the contrast between very intense light colours and very subtle dark colours next to each other.

Dark sky colour flooded with several blues.

Glazed colours defining sharp edges of mountains.

First wash on white paper.

Dark, wet trees painted onto damp background.

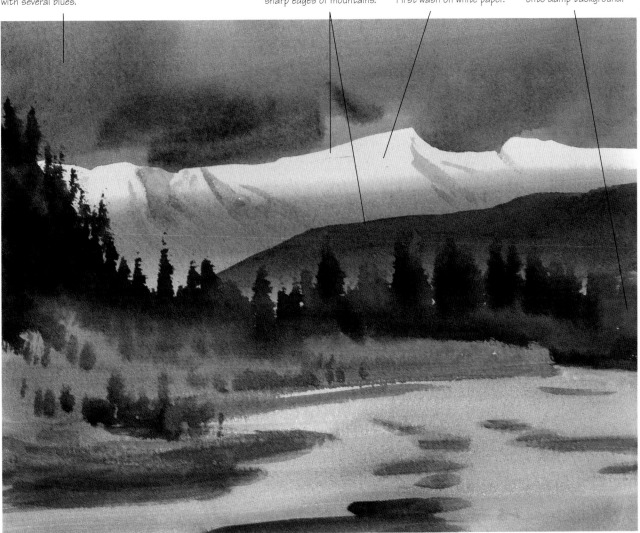

My palette was the most important component of this study. The sunlit top of the distant mountain and its reflection were painted with a light wash of rose madder and gamboge yellow. The shaded portions were glazed with two dark layers of magenta, phthalo green, and rose madder in varied dominance.

CHAPTER 6

Painting Demonstrations: A Step-by-Step Gallery

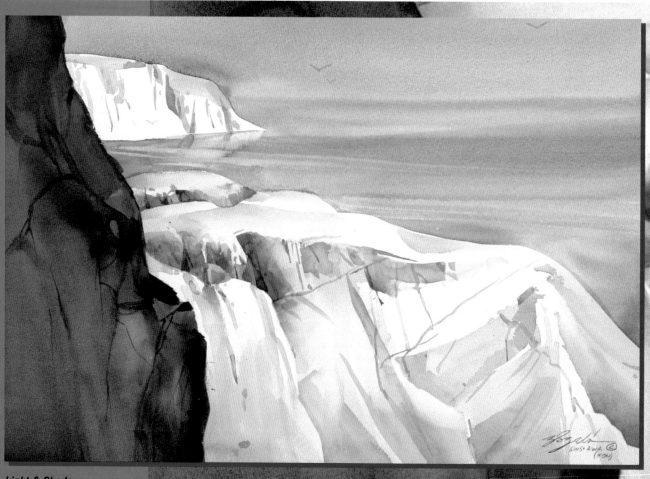

Light & Shade
34.25x44.5cm (13½x17½in)

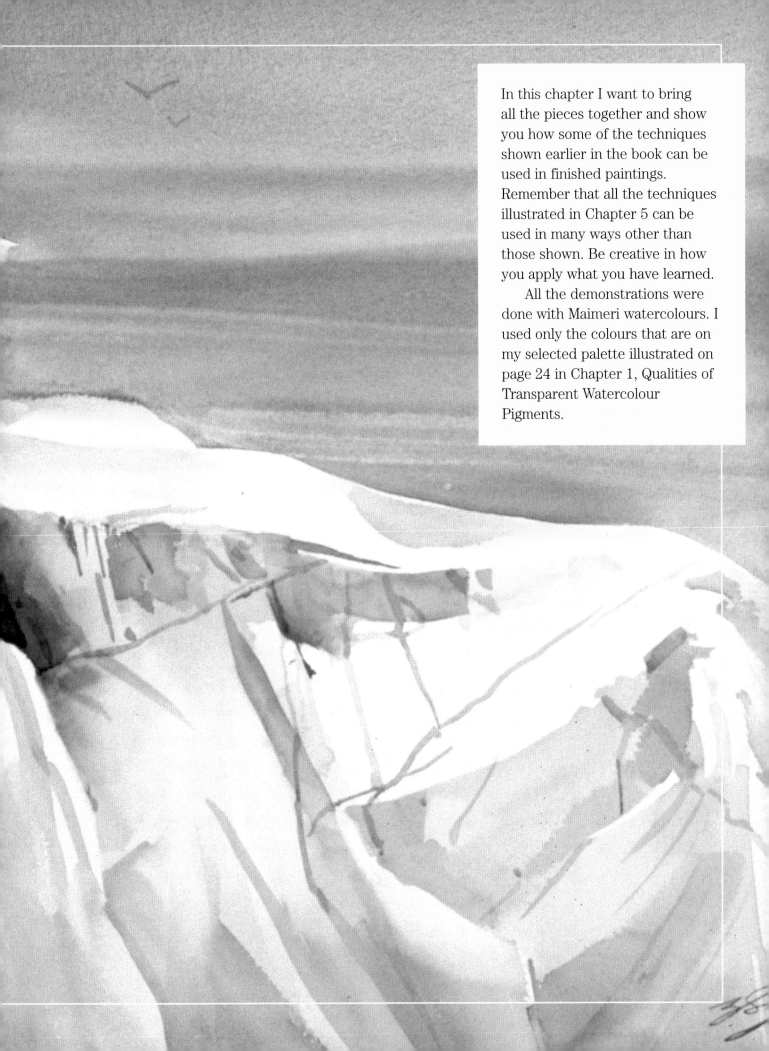

In this chapter I want to bring
all the pieces together and show
you how some of the techniques
shown earlier in the book can be
used in finished paintings.
Remember that all the techniques
illustrated in Chapter 5 can be
used in many ways other than
those shown. Be creative in how
you apply what you have learned.

All the demonstrations were
done with Maimeri watercolours. I
used only the colours that are on
my selected palette illustrated on
page 24 in Chapter 1, Qualities of
Transparent Watercolour
Pigments.

Flowers
Glazing with Staining Colours

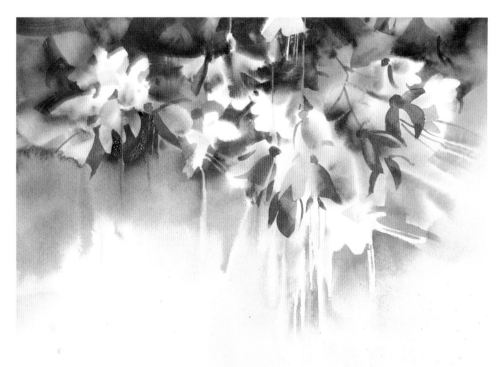

1 I started by wetting my paper, then flowed in the colours of my future flower clusters with quinacridone violet and rose madder. Around these soft reddish shapes I left lots of white negative spaces by painting around them with the cool, medium-tone background. My colours varied from cyanine blue to phthalo blue, cadmium green to brilliant yellow. My blues and greens and rose madder are staining colours, so I made sure they were interestingly located because they couldn't be removed after they dried.

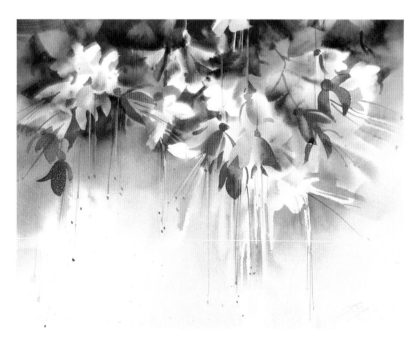

2 After the paper dried, I glazed some of the luminous, richly coloured, darker background shapes, carefully leaving out many negative contours of the flower clusters. I continued with more glazed details, expanding my positive shapes. Against the light background, I painted a few shaded purple flower silhouettes. The drooping stamens were painted with my small rigger brush, which is designed to do long, thin lines exactly like these delicate calligraphic strokes.

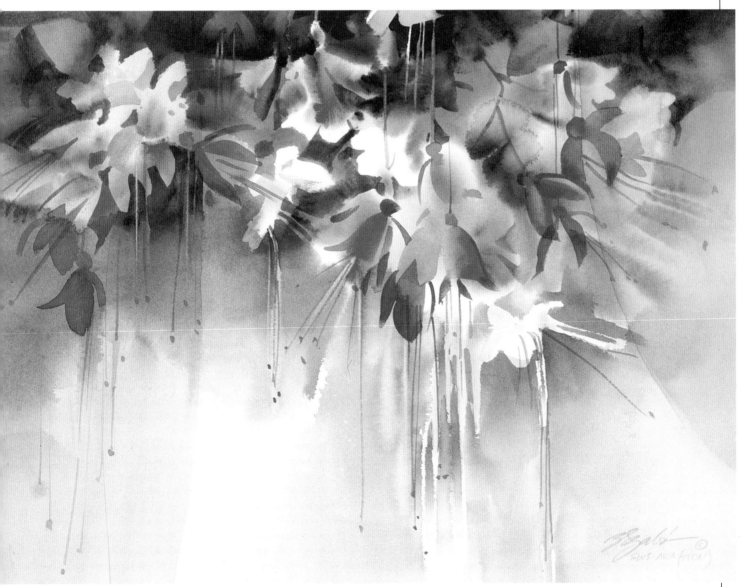

3 To balance the composition, I needed large subtle shapes. So I glazed a pale neutral mix of phthalo green and quinacridone violet on both sides of the painting. The curving edges echo the other curvilinear shapes, but the gentle tone reduced the overwhelming strength of the white at the bottom edge. The largest flower cluster became the centre of interest with a lot of visual energy concentrated in it because of the highest contrast there.

Bells of Love
35x45.5cm (13¾x18in)
Noblesse cold-pressed paper.
Collection of Dr Jane
O'Ban Walpole.

Icy Creek
Glazing and Lifting

1 First, I raised the top of my paper up about 2.5cm (1in) so it wasn't sitting flat. Then I started at the top edge of my dry paper using my 5cm (2in) bristle brush loaded with a pale mix of cobalt blue and burnt sienna, varying the two colours' dominance. Using the same two colours plus a touch of magenta, I established the silhouette of the creek. I started at the top and carried the beading wet wash downwards as fast as I could, gradually changing from a darker blue to a lighter, warmer dominance. With this positive shape, not only did I design the creek, but I was able to determine the edges of the neighbouring negative shapes of the snow-covered land.

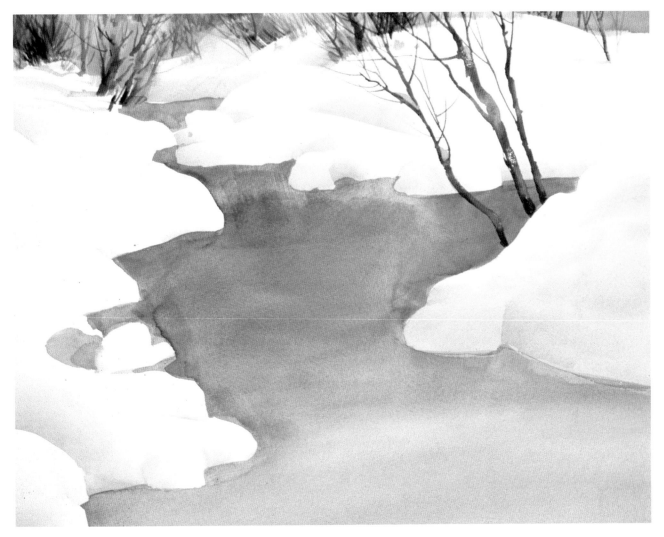

2 The rolling humps of snow were defined with shaded washes by leaving the peaks of each mound pure white and gently shading their near side. To define these white edges, I painted them with a rich mix of cobalt blue and burnt sienna and immediately blended away the top edges with a thirsty 2.5cm (1in) bristle brush. After these washes dried, I glazed in the distant shrubs and trees with a combination of cadmium lemon, burnt sienna and magenta.

To add the closer trees, I lifted out the background of the trees from the dark blue creek shape to allow the warm colour to shine with clear brilliance. I used the same colours as before, but painted the wider trunks with a soft, flat brush and the thin branches with my rigger.

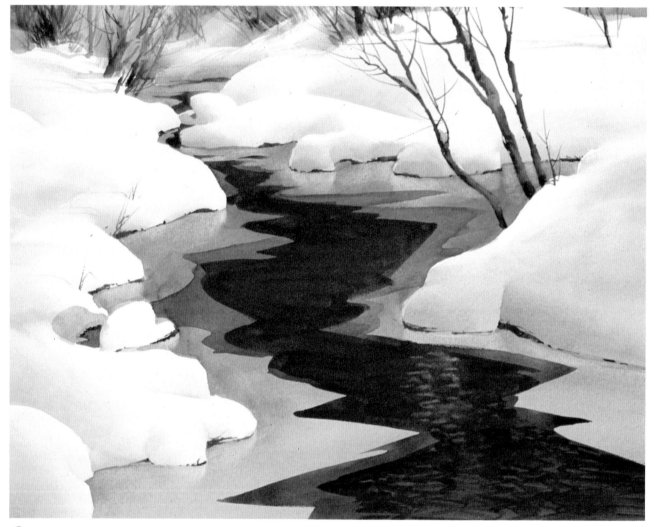

3 To show the ice forming along the edges of the creek, I glazed in slightly darker tones of burnt sienna, cobalt blue and some phthalo green. This glaze was dominated by the cool colours in the distance and by burnt sienna near the bottom. After it dried, I painted the dark water in the centre of the creek with a rich liquid glaze of burnt sienna, phthalo green and magenta, then lifted out the reflecting shimmer of the waves using the wet-and-blot technique.

The last detail was the reflections of the snowbanks in the ice. I moistened the shape of the reflection, loosened the pigment with a soft, flat brush, and blotted off the released colour with a tissue.

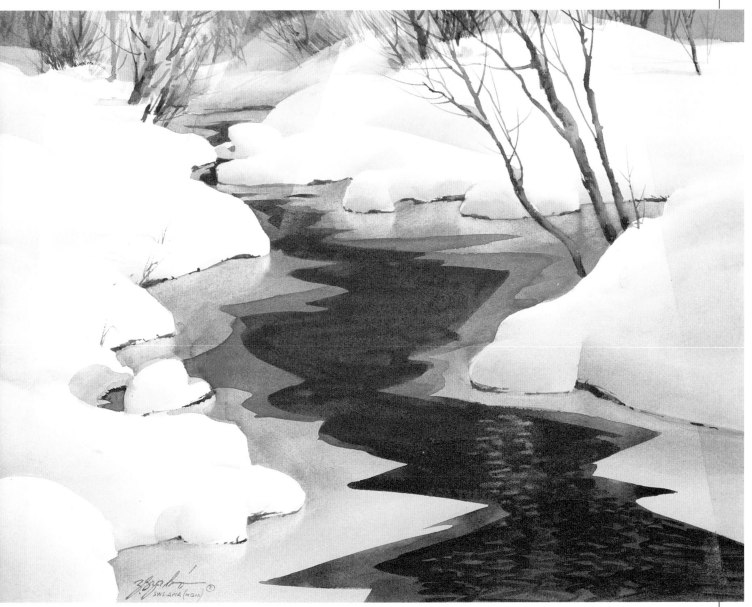

4 Because of the overwhelming dominance of curvilinear shapes, and as a complement to the energetic rhythm they represent, I wanted to add a stabilizing effect to the painting. I glazed a few pale shapes with my soft slant brush right over the completed details. I made sure that my colour was extremely transparent by using phthalo green and magenta (two highly transparent colours) heavily diluted with water. Because of the runny condition of my colour, I painted the shapes in only one careful pass. This last step also had the effect of strengthening the brilliant white of the snow.

Frozen Assets
35x45.5cm (13¾x18in)
Noblesse cold-pressed paper.
Collection of Drs Jack
and Teresa Flippo.

Shadows on Wood
Staining Texture and Lifted Sunlight

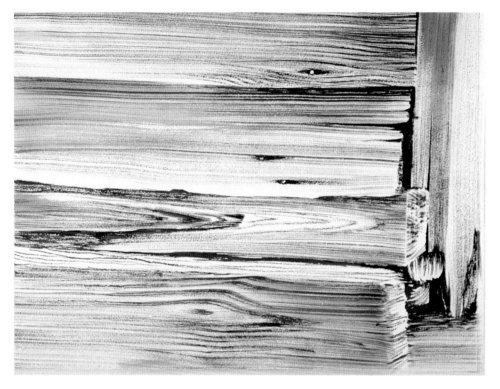

1 On a dry surface, I masked out each board to allow individual designs to develop. I filled my 5cm (2in) bristle brush with a mix of phthalo blue and ivory black because of their strong staining quality. I painted a dry brush stroke through the length of my boards, one at a time. This dark line pattern was enhanced to look more like wood grain by using a round brush and a rigger. The calligraphic patterns were united with a dark line between the boards. I added a staining green colour of hinted moss with cadmium green and phthalo blue.

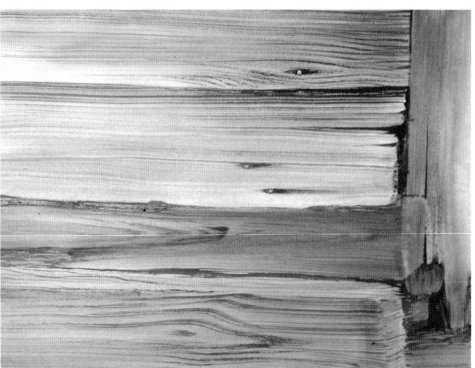

2 With my 5cm (2in) soft brush, I glazed the shadow colour over the entire area. My colour combination was burnt sienna, raw sienna and ultramarine blue in similar tones but differing in colour dominance. A word of caution: the wash was dominated by ultramarine blue, a reflective colour. Reflective colours alone or in a mix dry even lighter than do the more transparent pigments. Make sure that you paint them darker than what seems right while the wash is wet, in order to end up with good contrast between sunlight and shadow.

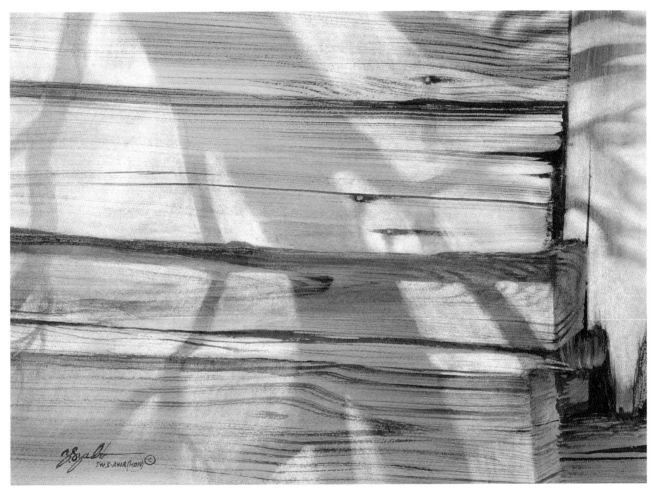

3 It was time to lift out the patterns of sunlight. Using my small bristle brush loaded with clean water, I loosened the colour on a small area next to the shadow, then blotted with a clean tissue. (It is very important to keep changing tissues between lifts. Freshly lifted colour can be pressed into the paper if you try to blot out a scrubbed colour with a dirty tissue.) After the sunlight was lifted out and the shadow was established, with my rigger I repainted the dark cracks wherever they were scrubbed off. I also moistened the area next to the nails and dropped in a soft, burnt-sienna brush stroke to indicate rust stains on the wood.

Autumn Colours
Controlling Edges

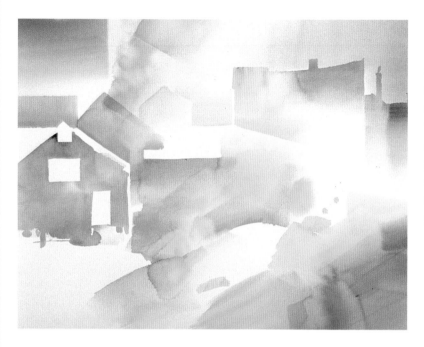

1 I began by painting some of the static shapes of the buildings with neutralized colours: phthalo green, magenta, phthalo blue and cadmium green. I also painted the small area of the visible sky with graded washes in the two top corners. While these forms were still damp, I began the colourful foliage of the foreground tree. For these glazes I used well diluted cadmium green, cadmium lemon and magenta on the light tones but added phthalo green to the lower-right corner.

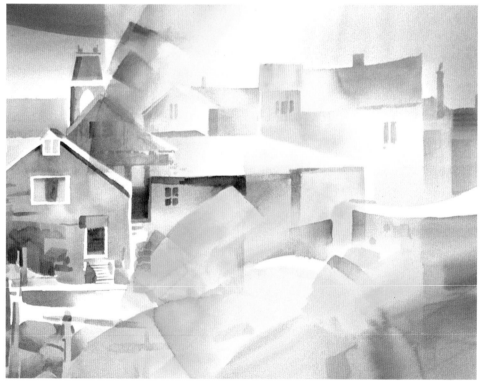

2 I further defined the character of the buildings using the same colours as before but in a slightly darker tone. I also added some windows, doors and steps with my flat brush. Using just magenta and phthalo green, I painted the rocks and fence posts in the lower-left corner. I also started to sharpen and develop the repetitive foliage units of the tree. By strengthening the contrast, depth was becoming more apparent.

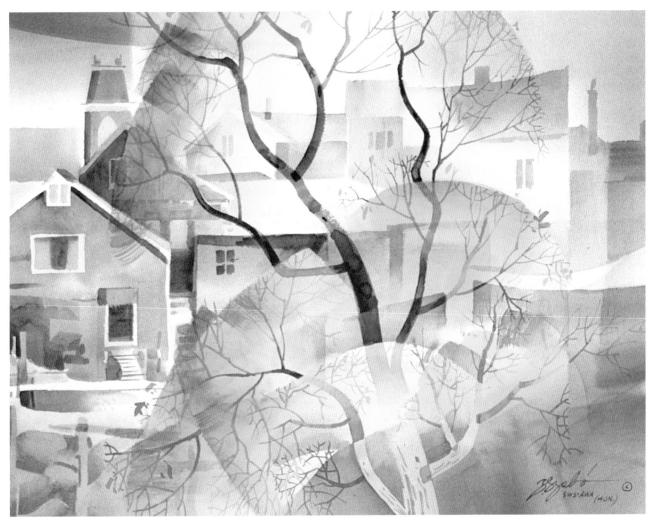

3 Finally, I turned my attention to the big foreground tree. At the bottom I started the trunk as a negative shape. As it moved higher, it turned positive and got darker as well beyond the filtering light of the pale yellow foliage shape. The powerful contrast of the skeleton of the tree clarified its location in space. I painted the small branches and twigs with the dominant colour of the foliage they were part of. These thin lines and the few leaf shapes were painted with my rigger. The strength in the painting comes from the harmonious colour and tonal relationship of the softly blended, yet contrasting, shapes.

Peace Town
35x45.5cm (13¾x18in)
Noblesse cold-pressed paper.
Collection of Scott
and Cindy Parker.

Misty Day
Wet-into-Wet Reflections

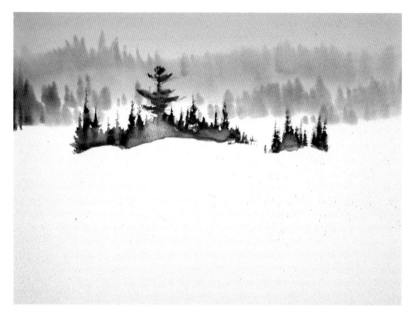

1 I started by wetting the top third of the paper, making sure that it was saturated and shiny. With my 5cm (2in) bristle brush, I painted the sky with a combination of raw sienna and cobalt blue. Into this wet background, I painted the two rows of distant, misty evergreens. After this wash dried, I painted the dark silhouette of the evergreens on the islands, using a dark but liquid wash of phthalo blue, burnt sienna and magenta. I painted the area fast enough to allow the wash to stay wet. Then I changed to my soft, flat brush and flooded the wash with wet, pure colours in different spots: magenta here, raw sienna there and a bit of cobalt blue, too, giving the shapes exciting colour variation.

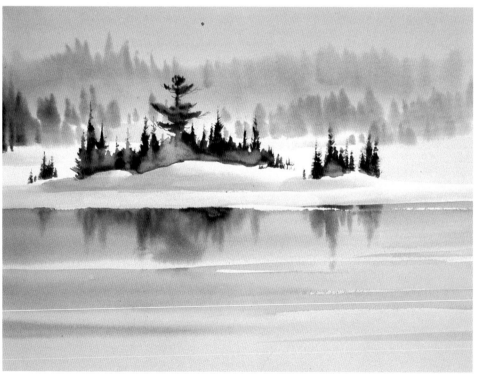

2 Now it was time to establish the shapes of the melting snow puddles. I filled my soft slant brush with a medium-tone grey mixed from cobalt blue and burnt sienna, and brushed on the horizontal shapes fast but let the edges stay broken like snow. Immediately into this wash I painted the dark, blurry reflections of the trees in a lighter tone than the trees but darker than the puddle's colour. I repeated the first glaze near the bottom, showing horizontal sharp edges as well as some soft ones. For the finishing touches, I completed the dry-brushed branches on the trees with my little rigger.

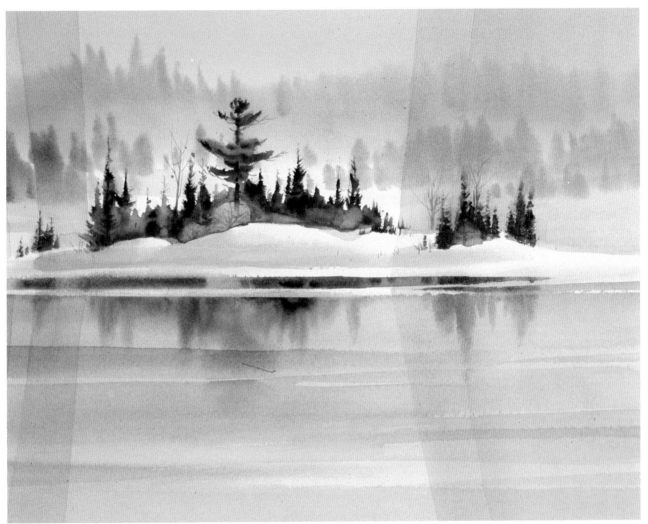

3 I felt that the overwhelming horizontal dominance of the large shapes needed a little boost, so I designed some light glazes over the two sides to attract the viewers' attention and to increase the impact of the whites and the bright colours in the dark shapes. I lightly brushed on these glazes with my soft brush in a wet condition, passing over the dry details only once. Repeated passes may blur or remove the otherwise dry colours. With these last pale glazes, the personality of the composition also gained individuality.

Winter Vanity
35x45.5cm (13¾x18in)
Noblesse cold-pressed paper.
Collection of Patricia B. Floyd.

Fallen Timber
Emphasizing Texture

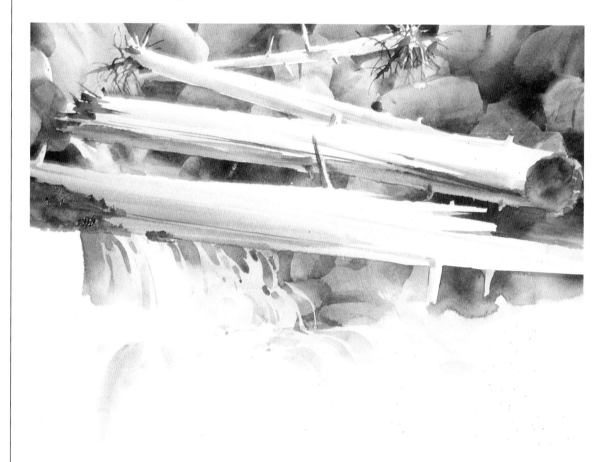

1 Starting on dry paper, I painted round the negative shapes of the crisscrossing logs, using my 5cm (2in) soft slant brush, which holds a lot of water and has a sharp point on its long-hair end. The turquoise wash for the water was a mix of ultramarine blue and phthalo green. On the bleached logs I added some raw sienna.

With my No. 8 round brush, I added darker glazes to the flowing water, indicating movement with the rolling shapes. Ultramarine blue, phthalo green and a touch of raw sienna were my colours. For the base washes of the rocks, I mixed burnt sienna, ultramarine blue and magenta in varied combinations. The sharp edges were left alone, but I lost the blended edges with a 2.5cm (1in) bristle brush. I also built more contrast on the logs by darkening the shaded sides, the broken ends and the dark roots with my No. 3 rigger.

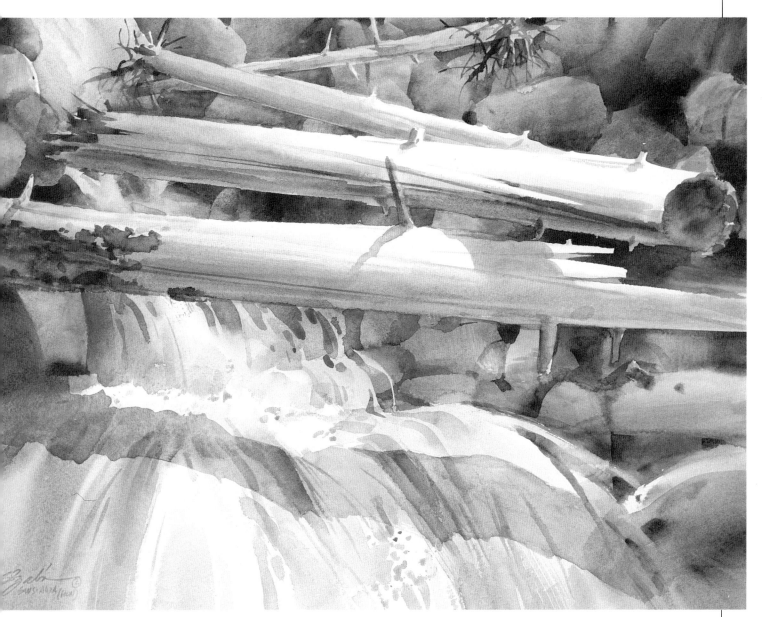

2 Next, I concentrated on the texture and the details. The lower part of the water-fall and the lower rocks were painted similarly to the upper ones, but the shapes were increased in size to show perspective. I also shaded the distant falling water, the rocks and the far end of the logs with a dark glaze of phthalo green, ultra-marine blue, magenta and a touch of burnt sienna. I used the same colours to paint the cast shadows on the logs as well as on the falling water in my foreground. For these glazes my 5cm (2in) soft brush was ideally suited, because it holds lots of liquid and my colours had to be light in tone and wet.

In a Jam
35x45.5cm (13¾x18in)
Noblesse cold-pressed paper.
Collection of Ruth
and Jack Richeson.

Fishermen's Shacks
Negative Shapes as Focal Point

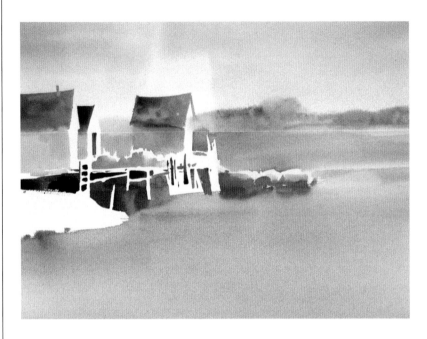

1 The background was painted fast enough with large wet washes to achieve a wet-into-wet effect. For the sky, the distant trees and the water, I used a delicately varied combination of cobalt blue, quinacridone violet and raw sienna. The razor-sharp edge and fine-pointed tip of my soft brush allowed me to paint round the white parts of the structures in the middle ground. When the background dried, I switched to my 2cm (¾in) brush and painted the roofs and walls of the buildings as well as the rocks and the dark space under the platform. Then I flooded them with individual colours while the washes were fresh and wet, creating colour excitement. The white negative shapes now took on the distinctive characteristics of light structures.

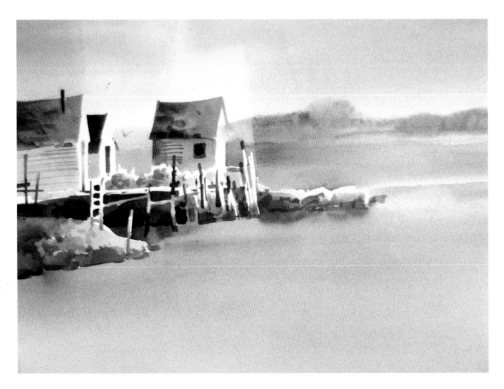

2 I continued with further light washes, detailing the rocks, the wooden structures, even the texture on the buildings' walls with my flat and rigger brushes. The dark tones of these shapes were achieved with separate glazes over dry washes in order to create more variations in colour, tone and texture.

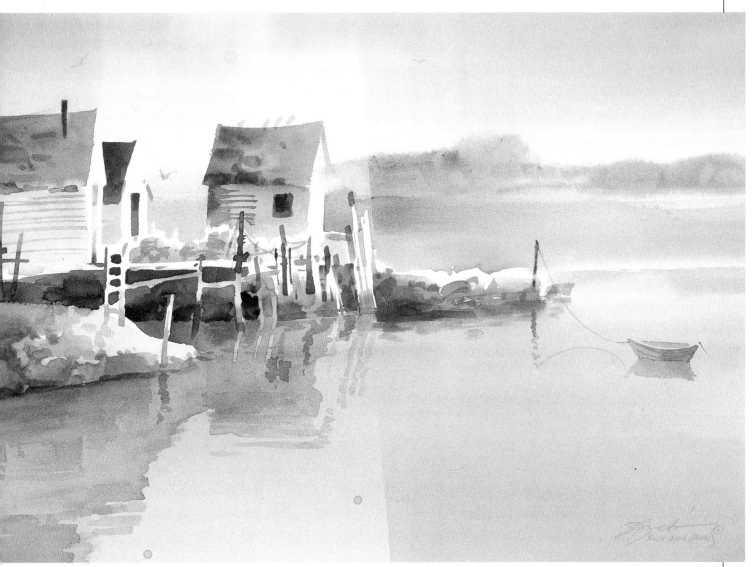

3 Finally I was ready to paint the reflections. Remember that reflections must relate to the reflected objects *as you have painted them*. For the colour of my reflections, I used the colours of the reflected objects added to the local colour of the water, which was a medium-tone grey. These colours were mixed with rose madder, raw sienna and cobalt blue.

To balance the overwhelming strength of the left side of the composition, I tied a little boat to the rocky point. It and its reflection added a touch of interest to the right side. To emphasize the whites of the focal point, I finished the painting with a very delicate, pale vertical glaze over the right and left sides. This delicate curtain effect added a personal accent to the painting that is purely emotional in nature.

Fisherman's Sunday
35x45.5cm (13¾x18in)
Noblesse cold-pressed paper.

Sand Dunes
Granulating Washes

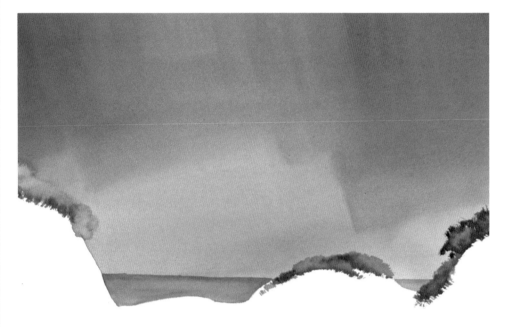

1 I thoroughly saturated my paper with water. With my 5cm (2in) soft brush, I worked in my dark sky. The blending of the edges was controlled by the timing and the proper amount of water in the brush. I also painted the water exposed behind the carefully protected edges of the dunes. My colours were phthalo blue, cadmium green and raw sienna. As the horizon touched the sky, the paint was barely moist so the edge is a little soft.

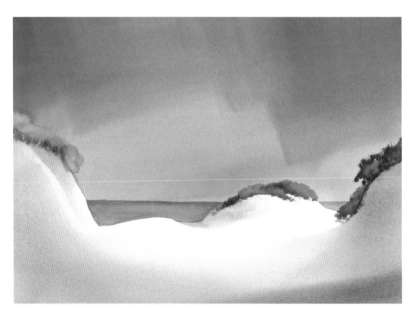

2 Because the paper had dried, I moistened the white foreground with clear water. With my 5cm (2in) soft brush loaded with a rich mixture of raw sienna and ultramarine blue (two very heavy sedimentary colours), I painted the very wet washes of the sand, leaving the contrast to the whites in the middle ground. These washes had to be painted with fast, determined brush strokes and then left alone so that the separation of the granulating colours was not disturbed.

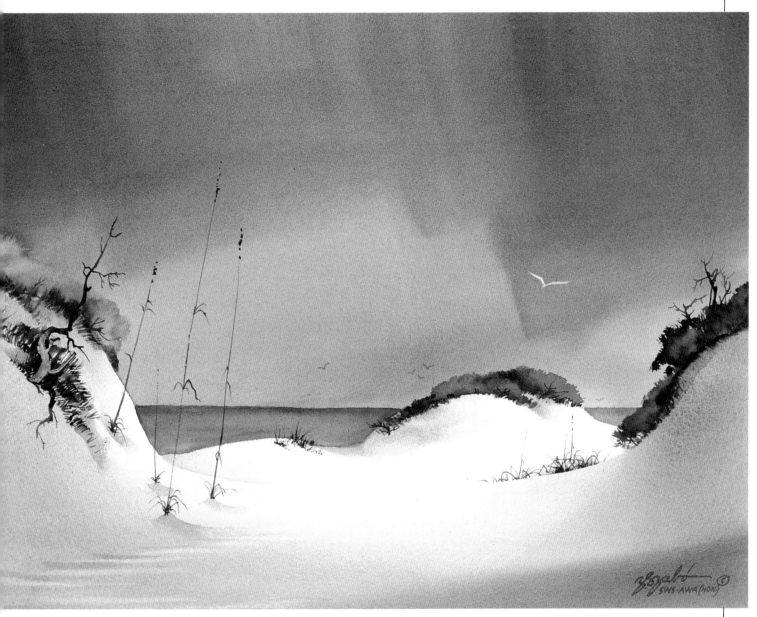

Scouting
35x45.5cm (13¾x18in)
Noblesse cold-pressed paper.
Collection of Jerry McNeill.

3 I switched to my 5cm (2in) bristle brush to paint the patches of shrubs at the tops of the dunes, using plenty of raw sienna, cadmium green, ultramarine blue and phthalo blue.

After these larger green shapes were secure, I switched to my small rigger brush for the remaining calligraphic details. The delicate shapes of the sea oats and the broken-down tree skeletons were worked with raw sienna, quinacridone violet and phthalo blue. Next, I proceeded with the rippled sand in the left foreground. First I wet-lifted the light sides of the ripples, then I painted in the darker sides with the previous sand colour. Finally, I lifted out the white gull by using a masking-tape stencil on the dry surface and wet-lifting the exposed shape of the bird. I blotted off the wet colour immediately and then removed the tape slowly and carefully to avoid tearing the paper surface.

Forest Rapids
Wet-into-Wet Technique

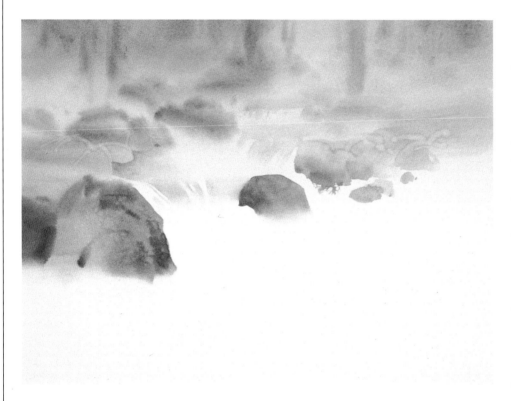

1 I saturated the paper with water, then spread a light wash of cobalt blue and raw sienna along the top area. I used my 5cm (2in) flat, soft brush, moving it horizontally from one side of the paper to the other, back and forth. As I expanded it downwards on the wet paper, I gradually lost colour completely. Switching to my soft, flat brush, I dropped in the distant tree and rock shapes. In the middle, I painted the two larger rocks with cadmium green, magenta, cobalt blue, and a little burnt sienna and splattered their wet shape with clear water to texture them.

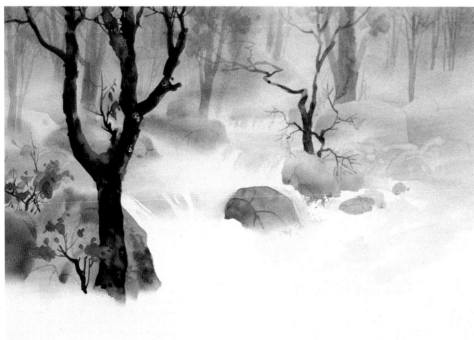

2 After the paper dried, I worked on the larger rocks and trees using a slightly darker colour mixed with burnt sienna, a little magenta and the dominant cobalt blue. I dropped in the two darker trees with my soft, flat brush. My darkest colour was mixed from burnt sienna, phthalo blue and magenta, and flooded with cadmium green, cobalt blue and raw sienna. I also painted the little shrub in front with the same colours.

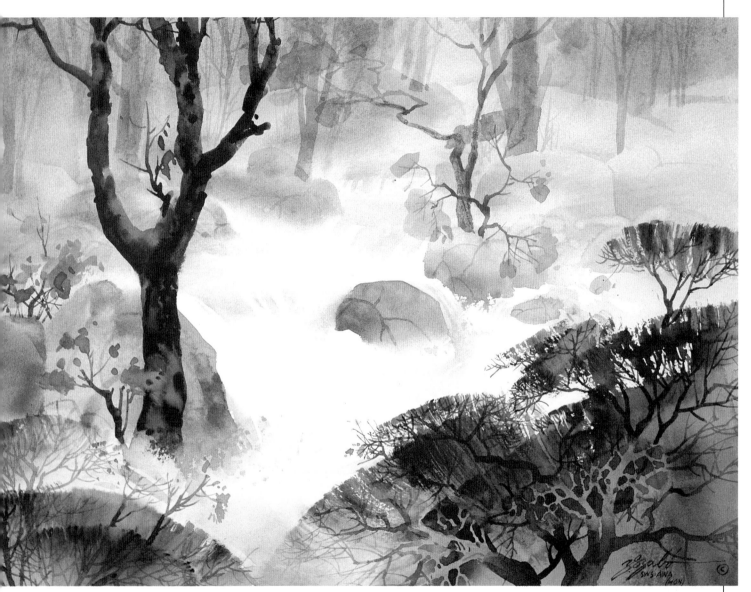

3 To complete the illusion of misty distance, I had to darken my foreground. I painted the drybrush foliage of the shrubs with my 5cm (2in) bristle brush, using dark mixes of burnt sienna, phthalo blue and cadmium green. I also enhanced the warmth of the big rock behind the large tree with a light glaze of magenta. The rough water under the big rock is a blended wash of cobalt blue and some burnt sienna. As this wash was drying, I splattered clear water droplets into it to indicate bouncing water beads. Because the composition is dominated by curvilinear shapes at the bottom and static shapes at the top, the illusion of distance is a little clearer.

Forest Rapids
35x45.5cm (13¾x18in)
Noblesse cold-pressed paper.
Collection of Ruth
and Jack Richeson.

Mountain Meadows
Palette Knife Technique

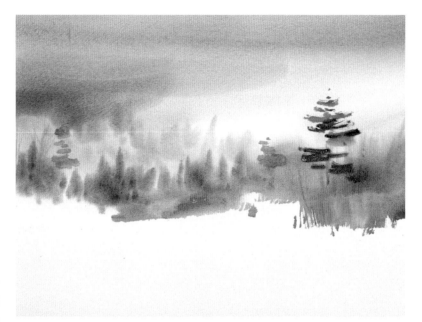

1 On thoroughly wet paper, I washed in the dark sky with my 5cm (2in) soft brush loaded with a combination of burnt sienna, ultramarine blue and some phthalo blue. Into the bottom of this wet wash, I added the distant frosty evergreens with a lighter mix of phthalo blue, ultramarine blue and a speck of rose madder. While the paper was still very wet, I painted in the darker and warmer trees in the middle ground, utilizing five colours varied in their dominance: phthalo blue, burnt and raw sienna, ultramarine blue and cadmium green. For the dark green foliage of my tallest pine trees, I held the bristle brush sideways and just touched the damp surface with the heavily pressed edge.

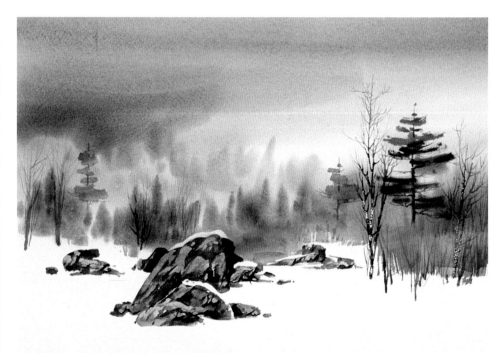

2 Onto the dry surface I painted the dark silhouette of the rocks with burnt sienna, ultramarine and phthalo blues and some rose madder in varying dominance. I painted these shapes in a thicker consistency than normal and immediately knifed off the lighter shapes on the rocks with my palette knife. This exciting texture is entirely the result of quickly applied paint and the fast knifing that followed. I also painted the delicate trees with my rigger brush filled with a dark combination of rose madder, burnt sienna and phthalo blue.

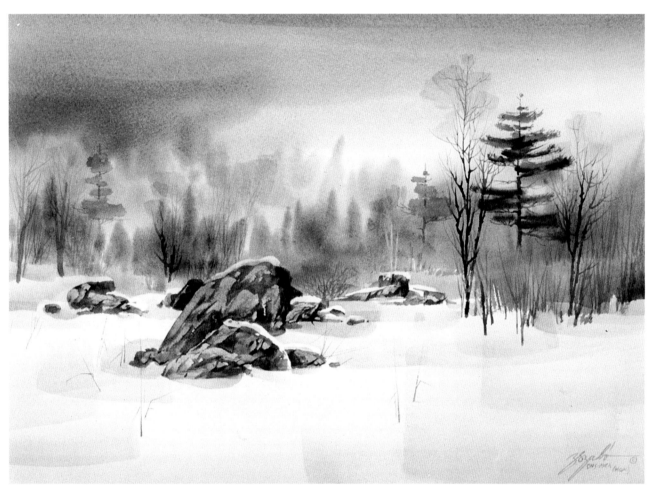

3 Next, I shaded the hollow dips in the snow with the lost-and-found edge technique. I used my 2cm (¾in) soft, flat brush to apply the smaller washes mixed from ultramarine blue, raw sienna and a touch of phthalo blue. I did the pale tones representing small twigs at the tops of the deciduous trees the same way, but left the top edges sharp. I completed the painting with the repetitive soft shapes in the foreground snow.

Snow Turtles
35x45.5cm (13¾x18in)
Noblesse cold-pressed paper.

Trees
Idealized Design

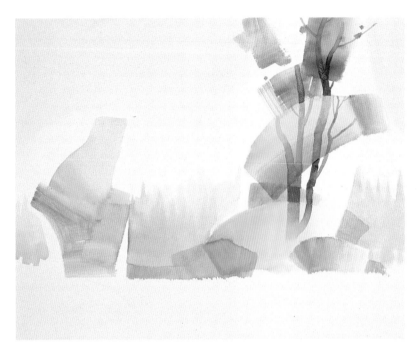

1 I started by wetting part of the paper with just a touch of cobalt blue and titanium white mixed wash, carefully avoiding the white paper behind the larger tree. While these washes were still wet, I applied the faint, distant evergreens with a mix of cobalt blue and a little burnt sienna. Next, I painted the rhythmical curvilinear shapes of the foliage clusters with colours dominated by brilliant yellow and accented with cobalt blue and magenta. I applied these basic shapes on a dry surface, and where the brush strokes overlapped another already dry shape, the colours doubled up in tone. I designed the larger tree's trunk and limbs following the same principles. The result is an exciting design that shows off watercolour's natural luminous glow.

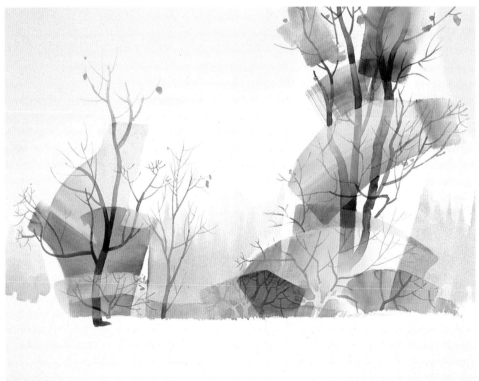

2 I continued with the rest of the branches, connecting the abstract foliage clusters with my 2cm (¾in) soft, flat brush for the wider limbs and my rigger for the smaller branches. On the lower shrubs, I treated some of the base branches as negative shapes by painting round them and leaving the background next to them darker. I also dropped in a few leaf shapes to indicate small accents. My colours were the same as in Step 1.

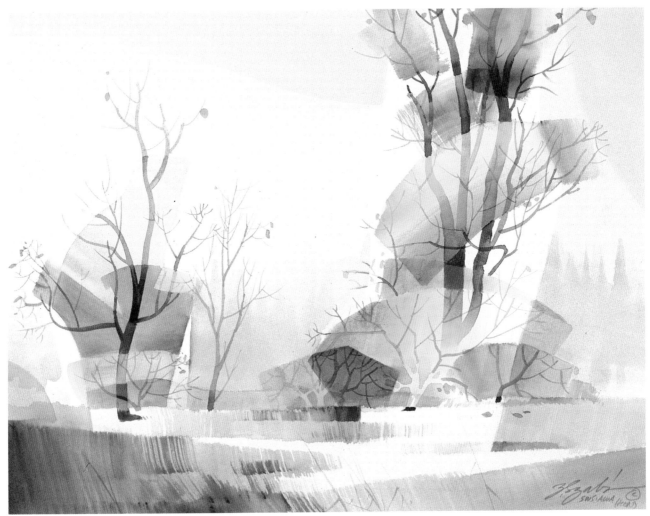

3 I was determined to preserve a sufficient amount of white paper next to my centre of interest, and to let this shape serve as a static complement to the tree's curvilinear design. The pale blue shapes along the top-left edge of the sky and the top-right corner echo the rhythm of the foliage. The shapes at the bottom of the painting, with their zigzagging straight edges, lead to the middle ground where the centre of interest is located. I painted these shapes with the 5cm (2in) bristle brush using cyanine blue and burnt sienna.

Autumn Couple
35x45.5cm (13¾x18in)
Noblesse cold-pressed paper.
Collection of the artist.

Quiet Harbour
Contrast and Reflections

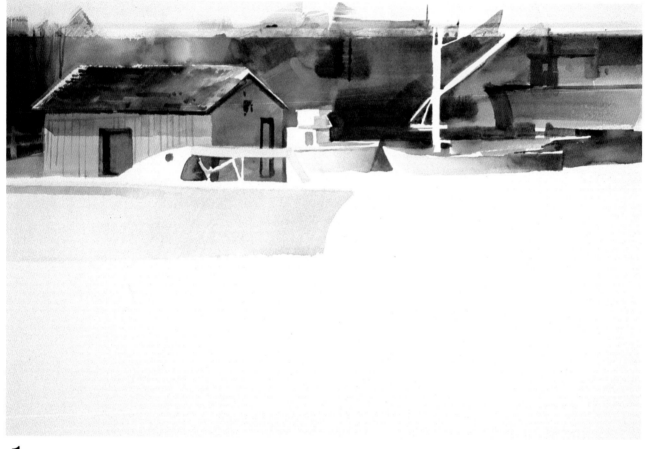

1 I began by roughing in the background and the boats with my 2cm (¾in) soft, flat brush, carefully painting round the white negative shapes. The white boats' hulls were modelled with a blue-grey colour mixed from cobalt blue and raw sienna, with a touch of phthalo green only on the boat with the white mast. The neutral dark background and the sunlit building's roof are a phthalo green and magenta combination applied in varying dominance. I also flooded this wet wash with a light tone of cadmium green and raw sienna to indicate future trees. For the foreground building's walls, I started with a pale raw sienna wash and, after it dried, I glazed the shadow with phthalo green and magenta in light tones.

2 Whenever your subject matter will include reflections, it is a good idea to
design first of all the elements in a painting that can influence the reflections,
because all reflections must relate to their originating objects. To paint the water and
the reflections where they belong, I washed in the basic local colour of the water
with a very wet combination of cobalt blue and raw sienna. Notice that at the bottom
half of the water, I let the raw sienna dominate to show the sandy bottom. Near the
smaller boats, I painted a little darker glaze round the reflections to hint at wave
movement.

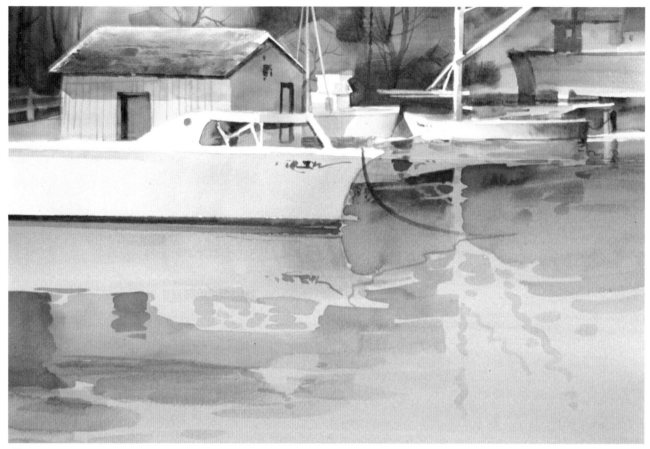

3 After my first wash dried, I raised the top edge of the paper to slant the surface a little. With the same colour combination, I glazed on the second tone of the water, avoiding the reflections of the light images. I made sure that the edges were established playfully as wiggly edges to indicate wave movement. I added a third tone to show where really dark images reflected. Notice that the reflections of the white boats are a little darker than the tone of the boats themselves, but the dark shapes in the background reflect a little lighter than their own tone.

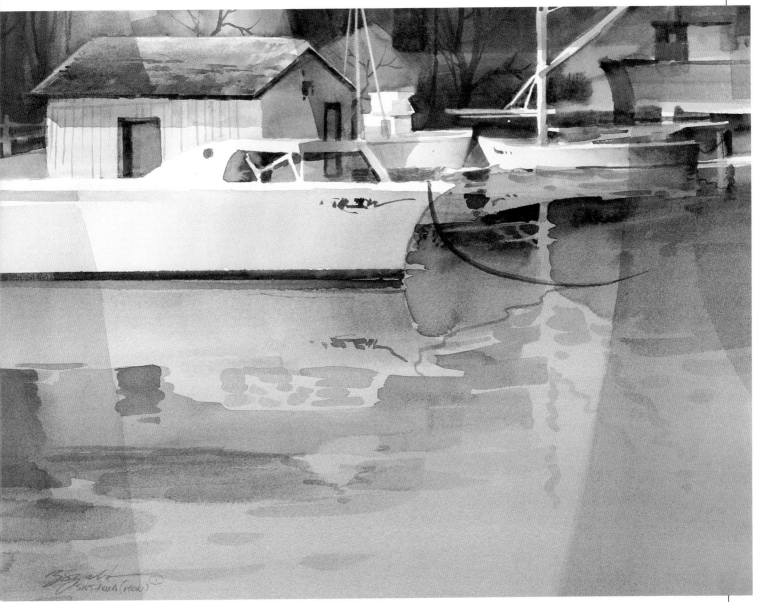

4 To all intents and purposes, the painting was finished. However, I felt the need for a unifying glaze to strengthen the composition on a more personal level. I glazed on the large transparent shapes over the dry details with just one pass, using my soft brush loaded with a wet mix of magenta and phthalo green in a very light tone. The neutrality of this colour enhanced the colour contrast in the untouched sections and boosted the impact of the whites, while adding to the personality of the painting.

Resting Harbor
35x45.5cm (13¾x18in)
Noblesse cold-pressed paper.

Daffodils
Backlighting

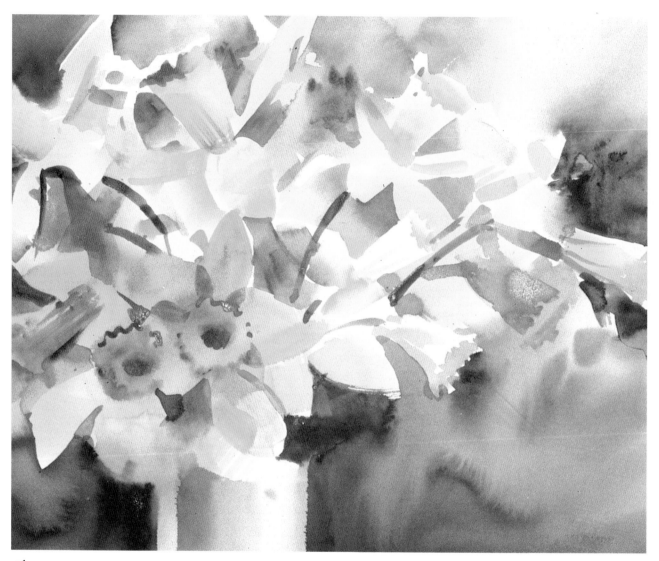

1 I started on dry paper, but to assure a loose, liquid technique, I painted with
lots of water in my washes. This way I encouraged the colours to mingle,
showing freely flowing washes with individual colour dominance. These washes
were applied with the 5cm (2in) soft brush. I carefully protected my negative
shapes, especially the white silhouettes. The light flower shapes were dominated by
cadmium lemon and brilliant yellow and a touch of burnt sienna. I defined the background with cooler colours. The darkest of these were dominated by phthalo green,
magenta and some burnt sienna. The overlapping tones created a textured excitement that subtly enhanced the painting's tactile qualities.

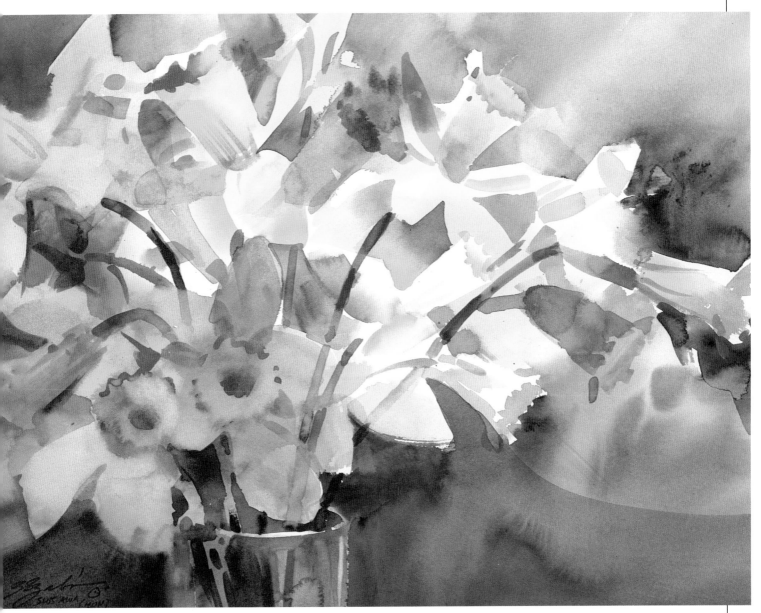

Golden Spring
35x45.5cm (13¾x18in)
Noblesse cold-pressed paper.

2 The dramatic illusion of strong backlighting is due to the importance of the carefully protected white negative shapes. To make the cool, dark background at the bottom of the painting even more dramatic, I glazed a light coat of phthalo green and magenta over the dry first wash on both sides of the vase. For the vase details, I used cobalt blue, phthalo green, burnt sienna and a touch of magenta. The highlights on the glass are negative shapes as well as lifted out. The daffodil petals' texture is a notable result of the sedimentary interaction of the cadmium lemon, the cobalt blue and the burnt sienna in a very wet wash.

Index